OPEN AND DISTANCE LEARNING SERIES

Teaching Through Projects

JANE HENRY

KOGAN PAGE
Published in association with the
Institute of Educational

Open and Distance Learning Series

Series Editor: Fred Lockwood

Activities in Self-Instructional Text Fred Lockwood
Exploring Open and Distance Learning Derek Rowntree
Improving Your Students' Learning Alistair Morgan
Key Terms and Issues in Open and Distance Learning Barbara Hodgson
Programme Evaluation and Quality Judith Calder
Using Communications Media in Open and Flexible Learning Robin Mason
Preparing Materials for Open, Distance and Flexible Learning Derek Rowntree

First published in 1994

Kogan Page Limited
120 Pentonville Road
London N1 9JN

Grateful acknowledgement is made to the Open University for kind permission to reproduce and adapt material on pp 102–6 from *The Information Search Guide 1993*, by C Hunter Brown and S Baker; the T401 *Study Guidelines 1992*; the T401 Search Profile Form; D301 *Brief Guide to Archives and Research Resources*; and *Libraries in the London Area*, 1979, by J Hawkins.

British Library Cataloguing in Publication Data

A CIP record for this book is available from the British Library.

ISBN 0 7494 0846 4

Typeset by BookEns Ltd, Baldock, Herts.
Printed and bound in Great Britain by
Biddles Ltd, Guildford and King's Lynn.

Contents

Series editor's foreword

The use of open and distance learning is increasing dramatically in all sections of education and training. This increase is occurring both in the UK and around the world. Many schools, colleges, universities, companies and organizations are already using open and distance learning practices in their teaching and training and want to develop these further. Furthermore, many individuals have heard about open and distance learning and would welcome the opportunity to find out more about it and explore its potential.

Whatever your current interest in open and distance learning and experience within it, I believe there will be something in this series of short books for you. The series is directed at teachers, trainers, educational advisers, in-house training managers and training consultants involved in designing open and distance learning systems and materials. It will be invaluable for those working in learning environments ranging from industry and commerce to public sector organizations, from schools and colleges to universities.

This series is designed to provide a comprehensive coverage of the field of open and distance learning. Each title focuses on a different aspect of designing and developing open and distance learning and provides concrete advice and information, which is built upon current theory and research in the field and how it relates to actual practice.

This basis of theory, research and development experience is unique in the area of open and distance learning. I say this with some confidence since the Open University Institute of Educational Technology, from which virtually all the authors are drawn, contains the largest collection of educational technologists (course designers, developers and researchers) in the world. Since the inception of the Open University in 1969, members of the Institute have made a major contribution to the design and production of learning systems and materials, not just in the Open University but in many other organizations in this country and elsewhere. We would now like to share our experience and findings with you.

In this book, *Teaching Through Projects*, Jane Henry draws upon her considerable experience in designing and evaluating project work in a variety of open and distance learning contexts. The major study she conducted within the Open University in 1978 proved to be a landmark, not only in the evaluation of projects across a variety of topic areas and academic levels, but in the analysis and interpretation she subsequently completed. The advice and assistance she has provided to project designers and learners, both within the Open University and elsewhere, has been significant.

In Section A, **Characteristics**, she puts the process of conducting project work in both a historical and an academic context. In Sections B and C of the book, **Process** and **Guidelines** respectively, Jane explains both the findings from individual studies and identifies those generalizations that may be applicable to your future project work. In doing so she provides you with a clear framework in which to present topics, provide advice on collecting and analysing data, estimating how much time different stages of a project typically consume as well as commenting upon learner support during the project work and its assessment.

The book is not just for those who design open and distance learning material that includes project work, even though these people will gain a lot from the book, but also for anyone engaged in teaching and for learning through projects. It will be of immense value to those planners, administrators and colleagues who are involved in the process of funding, organizing and supporting teaching and training. It will be invaluable to any learner about to embark on a project.

Fred Lockwood

Preface

Most educators and trainers recognize the merits of including project work in their armoury of teaching methods. Project work teaches and tests higher cognitive skills, it allows the student a measure of choice and responsibility for their learning, and as a consequence is a great motivator. The use of project-based learning is widespread thoughout education and training at most levels including primary and secondary schools, further and higher education, apprenticeships, in-service and professional training. The recent stress on access, enterprise and competences has increased the impetus to offer more relevant forms of education and the use of experience-based enquiry approaches such as project- and portfolio-based learning (Henry, 1989a). Simultaneously the use of open and distance learning has mushroomed.

While most educators and trainers advocate projects, their use in open and distance learning is often perceived as problematic. Many people doubt the practicality of offering this approach at a distance, as project work has traditionally been supervised closely. The extra support arises because the student is undertaking individual work and needs more help, guidance and monitoring than they would if undertaking a standard essay or report. In open and distance learning it is not always easy to provide the level of tuition and support project-based learning is assumed to require, especially when learners are geographically distant. Despite these practical problems there is a case for arguing that project work is a desirable addition to the open and distance learning curriculum, necessary to counter the charge that the pre-digested learning units (typical of open and distance learning) spoonfeed learners. They can also help motivate learners.

My most satisfying experience as an undergraduate was the completion of a major project. So some years later when colleagues from the Open University Project Study Group offered me the chance to undertake a major study of project work I jumped at the opportunity. This book builds on the fruit of that endeavour.

I began to investigate the practicalities and realities of undertaking project work at a distance in the late 1970s, through an extensive comparative investigation of over 4,000 students on 20 project courses. This study is referred to in the text as 'the OU study'. It aimed to examine the experience of those undertaking projects with a view to identifying principles of good practice. This study was unusual in that it compared students' experience of undertaking a project across many different disciplines from art history through ecology to systems.

During the course of this research it became apparent that the process of undertaking a project threw up similar pitfalls regardless of discipline, level and, to a considerable degree, project type. For example whether they were undertaking field projects, literature reviews or design projects learners showed similar generalized anxieties, a tendency to select topics for interest without due regard to their feasibility and to be chronically overambitious. Geology teachers underestimated the time learners required as badly as architects, biologists, educators, political scientists and psychologists. The study suggested a set of guidelines which intending project designers might find useful. I have had the opportunity to test out and refine these over the years and it is the results of this work which provide the framework for much of the thinking in sections B and C of this book. Presentations at various conferences have confirmed that many of the pitfalls described in the context of open learning projects apply equally to the use of project work in more conventional settings.

The book is divided into three sections. The first section provides background on the use of project work in education and training. Chapter 1 introduces the features that characterize project work and related activities. Chapter 2 examines the varieties of project work including literature reviews, information searches, empirical studies, experiments and design projects, and provides examples of projects from various disciplines. Chapter 3 offers a brief history of the project approach to teaching and goes on to describe some of the reasons for teaching though projects as well as their drawbacks.

The second section describes the process of undertaking a project through an examination of the difficulties typically encountered at each stage of project work. Chapter 4 elaborates on the problems associated with topic selection; Chapter 5 on the pitfalls that can occur during data collection; and Chapter 6 on the difficulties facing the student during data analysis and report writing. Chapter 7 outlines the key timing and scheduling aspects of project work. Each chapter also suggests ways of facilitating students' studies.

The final section offers guidelines. Chapter 8 discusses project design, material, audio visual and computer-based support. Chapter 9 compares several different approaches to assessing projects and discusses grading issues. Chapter 10 examines the tutor's role and outlines ways of maximizing this expensive resource. Chapter 11 discusses some of the very positive outcomes that are often associated with the use of project work and the question of drop out.

Some chapters begin with bullet-style summaries of the ensuing points and all end with a review of the areas covered and related questions to consider in connection with any projects you currently offer or are considering offering. Unless otherwise specified, the quotes are from participants in my various OU studies of project work. If I seem to quote my own work more than usual in a book of this kind, note that the OU project study is a rare example of cross-course comparison of project work and rarer still in evaluating the use of project work in open and distance learning. Much of the literature on project work is at the level of anecdotal case studies; for example, Adderley *et al.*'s (1975) attempt to bring together understanding about project work remains largely a collection of case studies. Exceptions to this rule include Benson and Allinson's (1979) excellent review of assessment procedures in engineering projects and several books advising students how to set about undertaking a project, for example, Howard and Sharpe (1983) and Jankowicz (1991). None of these, however, deals with project work in open and distance learning.

My desire to produce a book that is useful both to those who wish to concentrate on some particular phase of project work, such as project choice or data collection, and those who are interested in a particular aspect, such as workload, assessment or tuition, has led to some redundancy, which I hope is not too intrusive for those of you opting to read the text from end to end.

I have an on-going interest in project based learning and would be happy to hear from readers and researchers undertaking related work.

J Henry
Open University

Section A: CHARACTERISTICS

Chapter 1

Introduction

Project work usually offers the student some measure of freedom in deciding on the topic. It asks the student to undertake an enquiry process in which the students collect some material and then organize and present the data. Typically this involves an extended piece of work which the student often undertakes independently but in some cases is carried out with a group of fellow students.

Such an approach allows greater scope for the student to follow his or her own interests. He or she is allowed more control of the learning process. As a consequence many students get very involved in project work and find their motivation for undertaking learning increases. The increase in freedom granted to the student typically leads to an increase in the amount of tutorial guidance needed to help the student undertake the enquiry and the teacher takes on a different role, becoming more of a facilitator and adviser than pedagogue and expert.

This means project-based learning represents a very different approach from traditional schooling; instead of the teacher deciding what topics are relevant for the student and pre-digesting pertinent material for the student, projects give the students control of the topics they study and ask them to locate and make sense of material pertinent to the topic. The difference can be appreciated by representing traditional and project-based education as two extremes of a continuum:

Traditional education		*Project-based education*
Teacher selects topic	————	Student selects topic
Teacher supplies material	————	Student locates source material

Asking a student to select a topic, design a project, collect relevant data, organize material, analyse data and present the results is a demanding exercise requiring initiative. Many protagonists of this approach argue that it is essential for students to get their hands dirty with the process of enquiry if they are to develop higher cognitive skills like analysis, synthesis and evaluation.

However, there is a cost. Typically it takes an extended period of time for the student to go beyond merely gathering a few facts and organizing these into a coherent bit of learning. As a consequence, something else in the curriculum must go. There is often a tension between the desire to include as much as possible in the curriculum and the desire to ask students to complete a project that can deepen learning at another level.

Project work is also assumed to be harder to assess due to the difficulty the assessors are expected to have ensuring they are applying the same standard to projects on widely differing topics. There may also be disagreement as to whether the tutor who supervised the student throughout the exercise or an independent assessor is the more appropriate judge.

Nevertheless the use of project work is widespread because many teachers, trainers and academics believe it is necessary to motivate or stretch the student. Whether it is possible to offer project work at a distance is often thought to be a more open question but one addressed in the affirmative by this book.

Definition

There is no universally agreed definition of the term 'project' but the following six criteria act as a working definition:

the student –
i   (usually) selects the project topic
ii   locates his or her own source material
iii presents an end product (usually a report and often for assessment)
iv   conducts an independent piece of work (though there are also group projects)★

the project –
v   lasts over an extended period

and the teacher –
vi   assumes the role of adviser.

★Group projects generally require students to write up the work independently.

Adderley *et al.* (1975) point out that projects also involve a variety of educational activities, generally involve the solution of a problem and often offer the chance of tackling interdisciplinary areas.

A variety of terms are used to refer to different types of project-based learning. Examples include the *project exercise* which generally refers to a mini-project; *project component(s)* which covers one or more projects forming part of a larger course; *project courses* which are courses including a substantial project element; *project-based courses* which have all their assessment based upon a series of mini-projects; and *project credits* which are courses consisting entirely of one big project, similar to an undergraduate thesis or dissertation. Two other terms are worth mentioning: *project approach* generally describes a situation where project work is used as one approach among many, whereas *project method* (or *orientation*) refers to situations where institutions teach entirely or very largely through projects, offering students a discovery or problem-based approach to learning. Examples of the latter institutions include the University of East London's School for Independent Study, the University of Roskilde in Denmark, the University of Bremen in Germany, McMaster Medical School in Canada and much UK primary school teaching.

The term 'project' also has slightly different associations in lay and educational use. Though both groups think of projects as extended pieces of work with fixed time-scales for completion, to the lay person, especially those in business, a project is more likely to refer to a plan detailing the means of accomplishing a task, whereas for the educationalist it refers to an investigation carried out by the student in an area he or she selects, plans and subsequently reports on.

Degree of structure

A crucial feature of project work is the degree of structure, as indicated by the amount of choice given to students and the extent to which source material is provided or has to be located by the student. Some projects allow students a free choice of topic and expect students to locate all the material they need to complete it. In others the choice of topic is restricted and much of the material needed to complete the task is provided. I have found it helpful to distinguish between these two types of projects as unstructured and structured projects. Figure 1.1 shows project and related activities associated with each of these two groups. Some academics argue that the term 'project' is only correctly applied to the unstructured type, but the term is commonly used to apply to the structured type as well.

Structured project

Topic defined and materials provided
Case study
Project exercise
Structured project
Semi-structured project

Unstructured project

Student decides on topic and collects own material
Extended essay
Project component
Project-based course
Project credit
Project method

Figure 1.1 *Project continuum by degree of structure*

Unstructured projects tend to be allocated more time and a greater proportion of continuous assessment than structured projects. For example, in the Open University (OU) unstructured projects have been allocated anything from 20 to 360 hours and 2 to 8 assignments totalling from 3,000 to 12,000 words. By comparison structured projects are generally allocated between 10 and 40 hours and 1 or 2 assignments totalling 1,500 to 6,000 words.

OU studies provide further support for the validity of the unstructured/ structured project distinction as survey data from students on structured and unstructured projects generate a fundamentally different pattern of response and indicate that each requires a different level of support (Henry, 1978a & b). Some examples follow.

Unstructured projects

Unstructured projects are those where the learner designs, conducts, analyses and presents their findings on a topic of their own choosing using information they have located themselves.

For example, the teacher asks the learner to pick a building or group of buildings whose history is documented somewhere, frame a question concerning the building(s) and write a 5,000-word report to answer the question posed.

Structured projects

Structured projects are those where the topics are prescribed by the teacher (though the students may have some choice of options) and the methodology for collecting and analysing the information is also specified.

For example, the teacher provides the learner with a questionnaire and asks them to conduct ten interviews according to a quota sample. The learner sends those data to the teacher, who returns aggregate data for the student's locale. Each student is then expected to select one or more hypotheses to explore using those data and write a report on the findings.

Alternatively the teacher provides the student with a limited number of options. For example, Open University students studying the evolution course face a choice between 'salt tolerance in grass', 'genetic polymorphism in ladybirds', 'interspecies hybridization in angiosperm genera' or 'modelling natural selection'. The first three involve experiments or field studies and the fourth a computer simulation.

Semi-structured

There is a class of project that may more accurately be termed semi-structured than structured. Here, though the project area and methodology are prescribed, the nature of the work is such that students have a lot of responsibility.

For example, the OU personality and learning project offered learners 16 separate personality and intelligence tests suitable for various age ranges. Learners were required to select three of these to carry out a case study of an individual learner.

Real-world projects

A related distinction is that between 'real-world' and simulated projects. In the real-world project the student, or group of students, works with a real client to help solve a real problem, whereas in a simulated project the instructor provides the data on which students base their analysis.

In discussing projects in information science, Schuldt (1991) offers the example of setting up a database for a voluntary organization as an example of a real-world project. Usher *et al.* (1991) report on similar industrial group projects with local industry and government authorities. The idea of letting students undertake real projects may seem fraught with difficulty but Schuldt notes that users are 'extremely tolerant and very understanding of students' limited experiences', though she cautions that in the USA at least, instructors need to be aware of the legal liabilities that may affect the college where students undertake real projects.

Related activities

There are a number of related activities that constitute *borderline projects* where the student is still expected to organize material but most of it is supplied to the student, perhaps in the form of a file of cuttings or various papers. *Case studies*, where the topic is often set and some or all of the relevant documents are supplied, can merge into projects. In contrast, *extended essays* often give the student the freedom to choose their topic (often in consultation with the tutor) but draw on supplied or fairly straightforward secondary sources of information.

Figure 1.2 separates projects (on the right) where students are always required to locate some material, from borderline projects (on the left) where students are merely asked to organize material often supplied by the teacher.

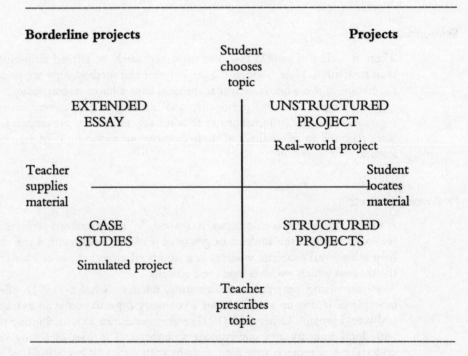

Figure 1.2 *Classification of 'real' projects and borderline projects*

Figure 1.3 offers a matrix summarizing the amount of freedom and responsibility placed on students in different project types in terms of topic choice, methodological approach and location of source material.

Project type	Topic	Methodology	Source material
Real world	Choice/ Limited or Prescribed	Choice	Locates own
Unstructured	Choice	Choice	Locates own
Semi-structured	Limited	Limited	Locates own
Structured	Prescribed	Prescribed	Some
Exercise	Prescribed	Prescribed	Provided
Simulated	Prescribed	Prescribed	Provided
Borderline	Limited	Prescribed	Some
Case study	Prescribed	Prescribed	Some or all provided
Extended essay	Choice	Prescribed	Locates own

Figure 1.3 *Summary of distinguishing features of project work and related activities*

Area

Projects are to be found in all disciplines. They are used to teach schoolchildren, especially young children, but also in further and higher education and adult training. More extensive use is normally made of them in applied disciplines and professional training such as engineering, architecture, design and agriculture. In Open University courses, certain disciplines, notably biology, geology, psychology, systems and research have made more use of projects over the last 16 years. These disciplines are either field based, heavily interdisciplinary and/or applied subjects.

A quarter of assessed Open University courses contained or consisted of project(s) in 1976, 1984 and 1992. In addition, almost a fifth of the remaining assignments were experiments of some kind. Case studies and extended essays were also used, but in under 5 per cent of the remaining assignments.

Project examples

The investigative methods used in projects are pretty constant across disciplines and at different ages. Like their peers in higher education, infant school children undertaking projects are quite likely to find themselves collecting information via direct observation, interviewing relevant individuals, undertaking experiments, collecting artifacts, and preparing some kind of report on the findings. Open and distance learning (ODL) projects employ similar methods, albeit at a different level of competence. The ODL projects described below indicate the range of possibilities (they are all taken from Open University courses).

History – students choose a topic in the period 1750–1950 related to one of the course themes: poverty and social policy, popular politics and élites. They undertake a national or local study of primary source documents relating to the topic.

Local History – students choose a topic in the general area of social science, formulate a hypothesis and test it by means of gathering historical data and analysing them quantitatively.

Public Administration – students undertake an enquiry into a topic in the general area of public administration using techniques of their choosing from within the limits of the approaches described in the course.

Developmental Psychology – either a case study of an individual child based on three tests or questionnaires, or a survey gathered from a group of 30 students aged 15 or older, using supplied questionnaires.

Social Psychology – three options, of which the student does at least one. The first involves carrying out five unstructured observations and writing a report on each. The second requires students to analyse the way in which men and women are portrayed in two newspapers by a content analysis and, if desired, a structuralist analysis as well. In the third, students explore their own attitudes to a group of people, using Kelly's repertory grid technique.

Curriculum – students are asked to select a school curriculum for analysis. Source materials in the form of a TV broadcast and booklet are provided for those who do not wish to select their own curriculum to study.

In-Service Teacher Training – of the seven options, four involve students in initiating and evaluating some aspect of the reading curriculum, one evaluating and suggesting improvements and two (intended for those without access to children) involve assessing reading material.

Ecology – the practical project work in ecology involves students in choosing a topic, designing and conducting an investigation and analysing and writing a report on the data in consultation with the tutor.

Geology – several broad areas are suggested. These involve producing a summary of existing data or a field guide, or testing a hypothesis by gathering original data.

Environment – the project requires the student to collect information on up to 20 manual workers via a questionnaire. The report involves a summary of the data and findings and a discussion of them.

Technology – students are sent a booklet giving details of an industrial accident, caused by mechanical failure. Students are required to report on the mode and cause of the failure and conditions that would have prevented the accident.

Level

In higher education, project work becomes more common the higher the level of study. It is often introduced late in the curriculum on the assumption that students need to have reached a certain level before they are capable of this kind of work. For example, in a survey of electrical engineering departments, Carter and Lee (1981) found that while experimental investigations were more common in the first and second years of study, three-quarters of practical work in the final year was devoted to projects. Similarly, Hoare's (1980) survey of chemistry courses showed that virtually all used projects and that one or two major projects generally occupied all the student's practical laboratory experience in the final year. Figure 1.4 shows that this pattern of more project work at higher levels is mirrored in the Open University's ODL projects. About two-thirds of the projects occur at the higher 3rd and 4th level courses and a third at the lower 1st and 2nd level.

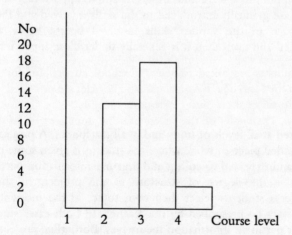

Figure 1.4 *Number of project courses by level*

Cornwall (1975, 1977) argues there is no good reason for the restriction of projects to post-second year students. And indeed I found that projects introduced in first and second level courses at the Open University were just as successful as those presented at the third and fourth level (Henry, 1978a). Early experience of a project may well help prepare students for projects in later courses. For example, Hodgson and Murphy (1984) found biology students undertaking a third level field-based project who had previously undertaken the second level course which included a field-based project performed slightly better than those who had not done so. Where projects are introduced throughout the curriculum it is more common to find structured projects at lower levels and longer unstructured ones at higher levels. Many disciplines use a project credit at the end of the student's period of study. Higher qualifications like M.Phils and Ph.Ds usually take the form of a thesis or dissertation – in effect, one huge project.

Since projects skills are standard across so many projects there is a good case for systematically introducing these throughout the curriculum and gradually increasing the level of difficulty of the projects offered. For example, offering project exercises like writing a report on a file of cuttings and asking students to add to this file from newspapers throughout the year, in the first year of study; then offering a structured project in the second year, a larger unstructured one in the third and project credit in the fourth. As it is students are often introduced to projects in their final year of study with little preparation. Perhaps project-based learning could take some lessons from the practice of apprenticeship. Unlike most project students, apprentices were and are given ample opportunity to observe what is expected, are gradually introduced to the skills involved and then given considerable practice in the various skills involved before being asked to undertake a 'project' and even then it is generally under close supervision.

Review

Project work is used at all levels of study and in all disciplines. A project may be defined as an extended piece of work where the student is given some choice in the topic studied and expected to collect and organize information pertaining to it. A key aspect is the degree of structure in the project. In the longer unstructured projects students select their own topic; in the more structured project the topic may be prescribed by the teacher. In both cases students are expected to gather pertinent information themselves. Borderline projects such as case studies ask students to organize information supplied by the teacher or trainer.

Points for reflection

What sort of projects are offered in your department?
How structured are they?
What scope can you see for offering related activities?

Chapter 2

Project types

The term 'project' is used to cover a variety of activities, which can be broken down into four fundamentally different types of inquiry: the literature review which normally entails research in a library; an information search which uses primary or secondary data; empirical research which might involve a survey or case study or an experiment; and design projects that involve specification and/or construction.

It will come as no surprise that certain varieties of project work are more common in some disciplines than others, namely:

- Literature review – humanities
- Information search – all
- Empirical research –
    Survey – social sciences
    Case study – education, management, systems
    Experiments – science
- Design projects – technology, art and design.

This link between project type and discipline is by no means a hard and fast rule; one finds science and technology students asked to do literature reviews and applied social scientists asked to design solutions to people problems.

Figure 2.1 indicates some common examples of each type of project. A discussion and examples of each type follow.

Literature review

Most of us will be familiar with that stock in trade of the scholar, the literature review. Indeed much teaching comprises the teacher's attempt at doing the literature review for the student. It has been argued that by so doing, the teacher

---

Literature review
  Newspaper review
  Field guide
Information search
  Primary source
  Secondary source
Empirical research
  Survey
    People
    Resources
  Case study
    Individual
    Organization
  Experiment
    Home
    Field
Design
  Specify
    Social
  Build
    Technological

Figure 2.1 *Examples of each type of project*

has done much of the learning for the student, thus spoonfeeding him or her with pre-digested information that does little to stretch his or her higher cognitive skills.

The object of a literature review is to counteract this charge and force the student to gather information and construct a piece of work from a variety of sources. This approach is central to much humanities research and a central element in all research, as it is important to check you are not reinventing the wheel.

Dissertation

Students are asked to write an extended essay drawing on a variety of material.

Politics – for example, students of politics are asked to submit a dissertation on some aspect of British foreign policy (of their own choosing), using a hypothesis and method of analysis drawn from the course set reading.

Field guide

Students are asked to produce a guide to local facilities and phenomena, such as local geology, historic buildings or flora and fauna.

Geology – for example, geology students were able to use the idea of producing a field guide to their area as a fall-back project if they lived in localities, such as East Anglia, where there were no hard rocks to study.

Training

Students collect articles from newspapers and magazines pertinent to a particular topic.

Newspaper scan – for example, students were asked to collect articles from general newspapers and magazines on a subject of interest to them. They were then asked to make a short presentation to other students on what they had learnt. This is in some sense a training project, which introduces students to the idea of looking at material outside that designated as part of the course. It also provides a chance to bring in topical material and relate education to the students' everyday life.

Information search

There are two rather different types of information search; the first draws on primary source material (ie, original data) and the second on secondary source material (ie, pre-digested material).

Primary data

Students undertake a project based on collecting data from records, documents and archives.

Local history – for example, a historiography course requires students to undertake a project on a topic of their choosing, that relates to one of three course themes. They would use sources like old parish registers, letters and documents held in local record offices and national archives. The object of the exercise here is to give students a feel for what is involved in 'doing' history.

Secondary data

Students undertake an analysis of information they obtain from reference texts in libraries or case study-type material supplied to them.

Statistics – for example, statistics students are asked to collect statistical data on various subjects, largely from reference texts held in libraries, and perform various analyses on them.

Training

A form of training that acts as an introduction to larger projects is to offer students a file of documents pertinent to a particular issue and ask the students to use this material to write a report on that topic.

Systems – for example, students are sent a file of various materials relating to an earthquake and asked to write a report explaining some of the reasons for the failure to predict this particular event.

Empirical research

Empirical projects ask students to base a project on an analysis of original data, often collected by the students. This may involve surveys, case studies or interviews and/or the use of assessment instruments.

Survey

Students may be asked to undertake a project which involves surveying people's attitudes or beliefs or measuring the incidence of some inanimate element such as noise or the numbers of cars, mice, etc.

People
Social science research – for example, social science students were given a questionnaire and asked to interview a small number of people, satisfying a quota sample, in this case individuals of a particular age, sex and type of employment.

Resources
Environment – students may be asked to measure variables indicating pollution levels in their area, for instance number of cars per hour, sulphur dioxide levels in local rivers and in the atmosphere, etc. These data can then be collated and make an ideal group project.

Case study

Case studies ask the student to make a more detailed study of one particular person, organization or issue.

Education – for example, education students were asked to pick an individual and draw up a profile of that individual according to certain criteria. In undertaking this case study students were required to use an aptitude test and personality inventory selected from a small number that were provided.

Management – much management teaching is based on case studies of particular firms and situations. Traditionally the student is given a variety of materials relating to a particular firm, including background on the context and competitors. They may be asked to present an analysis of the strengths and weaknesses of the firm or to offer proposals on an appropriate strategy given the particular conditions at that time.

A project goes beyond this paper exercise and asks the student to undertake an analysis that may involve site visits and interviews with staff as well as analyses of balance sheets. In open and distance learning this is often based on the student's own organization.

Experiment

Traditionally much science teaching is based on experiments, an approach which involves controlling the variables under scrutiny. ODL science teachers have been wonderfully creative in developing home-based experiments to substitute for traditional laboratory work.

Laboratory

Many experiments in science require specialist equipment and materials and some can be dangerous, so they are traditionally carried out in a laboratory set aside for this purpose. In ODL this type of experiment is often restricted to periods when students meet together with staff, for example at a residential school or tutorial.

Field

An alternative approach is to carry out an experiment in the field, in the outside world, sacrificing some of the control offered by a laboratory for more relevance and the extra ecological validity offered by 'real world' experiments.

Ecology – for example, ecology courses may ask students to compare carbon dioxide, noise or algae level at different times of the day or year and in different locations.

Home – it is possible to offer students simple projects to carry out in their own home.

Introductory science – for example, the Open University science foundation course asked students to do a small experiment that involved little more than mashing up bananas and placing them in a covered container in an airing cupboard for a few days and noting what emerged and when. If all went well a fruit fly might magically appear. The students' task was to observe what appeared and write a report about this mini-experiment. Over a period of 13 years in which the experiment was running, several new species of fruit fly were discovered.

Design

There are two kinds of design project: the first where students merely specify a plan for a design of some sort and the second where they go on to build whatever is specified.

Planning

Projects where students plan but do not build a design are common in architecture, town and country planning and landscape gardening. However they are also found in less obvious quarters like applied social sciences.

Community – for example, students have to identify an unmet social need in the community, present evidence to support their contention, and design in some detail a way of meeting that need and a means for evaluating the proposal.

Building

Building projects are common in engineering and manual skills training.

Engineering – in some cases students just simulate a design but in others students design and build a prototype to test its performance.

Project case studies

This section discusses some open learning projects from a variety of disciplines in a bit more detail. A description of a group-based, independent study and a school-based project are also included.

Humanities information search project

This project was part of a course covering architecture and design in the period 1890 to 1939. There were two project options, one of which was intended largely as a fall-back option.

The main project asks students to look for some building or group of buildings or design work which they could get access to for examination and which are documented somewhere. The project report takes the form of a 5,000-word essay in answer to a question which can be formulated with the tutor, for instance. 'How was the East South estate brought into being, what were the architects trying to achieve and how does it compare with similar ventures at this time elsewhere?' Students rated the project as very interesting but time-consuming.

Materials

The project guide provided the main support material for students. However some other case study material was intended as a model for the project, as the techniques needed for the project were demonstrated there. Some time at the course residential school was also designed to assist students with their project work.

Assessment

The project assessment involved three submissions. The first two were unassessed. First the students prepared a 500-word outline project proposal. Some months later the students were expected to submit a 1,000-word progress report and about six weeks after this the 5,000-word project report. The grading arrangements were such that the project assignment might count as three assignments or only one according to how successful it was. (See Mace, 1984, for a fuller account.)

Social science project exercise

The course investigated the nature of decision making in Britain, in such sectors as agriculture and health. Students were given an interview schedule and related background reading, and told to obtain five interviews and to use these together with other background data to investigate a pre-determined hypothesis selected by staff. Students sent their data in to staff by post, so a summary of all students' data could be prepared and posted back to students. The project was allowed an insuffient 24 hours of study time.

Materials

Extensive materials on how to interview, interpret data and write a report were provided. They included:

Interview schedules
Letters of introduction
Coding sheet
Advice on how to conduct the project exercise
Background information
Radio programme.

Assessment and evaluation

The project was assessed by an optional 1,500-word assignment which less than half of the students chose to complete.

Project-based research methods assignments

The course aimed to teach research methods to education and social science students. All the assignments were project-based. There were three projects: a qualitative research exercise based round two unstructured interviews with one individual and subsequent content analysis; a quantitative project based round statistical analysis of structured interviews, each student providing four of the interviews according to a quota and groups being supplied the aggregated data; and a research evaluation exercise comparing three supplied research papers.

Material

Extensive support materials were provided. For example, the survey project was supported by a 50-page survey guide, a statistics booklet, computing guide and other text explaining research design, questionnaire design and analysis, statistics, video material illustrating how to interview and audio material offering advice on statistical analysis.

Assessment

Four unassessed assignments provided training in the skills needed. Three further formative assignments acted as draft reports for each project, which were each assessed by a 3,000-word report. Initially each project was double-marked.

Education survey project

This course aimed to equip students with the knowledge necessary to evaluate research. The project aimed to provide 'insights and experience that you can only acquire by actually carrying out research'. The student was expected to collect and analyse questionnaire data from 30 school children. Students analysed their data but also made these available to staff for aggregation. Staff hoped this experience of doing the project would 'bring home lessons in other parts of the course'. The project was allowed an inadequate 31 hours.

Material

The course provided substantial back-up including a series of booklets designed specially to support the project, covering project orientation, project hypotheses, project instrumentation and project analysis. A radio and TV programme were used to inform students of the national data.

Assessment

The project was assessed by one compulsory assignment. Some help for pacing was provided by a calendar giving the dates when the students were supposed to read the various project material, beginning some six months prior to the date the assignment was due. There is some evidence that after the assignment was made compulsory the drop-out rate increased.

Management staged mini-projects

Open learning management courses typically base many of their assignments on the student's experience of their own organization rather than asking the student to write essays or prepare a report dealing with case study material. These experience-based assignments are in effect mini-projects, the relevance of which seems to increase motivation. The creative management course I chair provides an example. Feedback shows this approach to be very popular with students (Henry, 1992; Swift, 1992).

Material

On this MBA course, students receive a mix of distance study materials, comprising specially written text, set books, readers, video, audio, broadcasts, software and conferencing. Much of the course material supports the project assignments indirectly. In addition, the use of personality inventories and a TV broadcast support the first assignment; a residential school, written material, audio, video and software support the second assignment; text and TV the third; and a specially written unit of material supports the final project assignment. The course also includes guidance on literature searches.

Assignments

The four assignments can be linked so that they form a staged project that spans the course. The first assignment asks the students to compare their personal style and organizational climate and, arising from this, to pick an area they wish to develop over the course. The second asks students to use some group-based techniques to address a real problem (eg, the previously identified development area). The third requires students to apply course ideas to develop a strategy to address the problem and the fourth to go some way towards implementing this strategy in the work place. In effect the students are asked to act as internal consultants and their project report records their success or otherwise, together with reflections on and learnings from the experience.

Mathematics project

This project was aimed at maths teachers of children aged 8 to 13. The course philosophy advocated integrated teaching in which problem-based learning featured strongly:

> ... the content of learning must be geared to the interests and needs of pupils. This means that real needs and problems concerning their private and professional life, both present and future, have to be considered. Problem areas from reality will determine the content of teaching (Howson *et al.*, 1981).

The course designers believed that there is a lack of confidence in doing mathematics and that people do not consider the practice of maths as relevant to their lives. The course sought to show that these attitudes '... are in general misplaced because people use mathematics more than they realise, and ... might use it more often if they had more confidence' (Zand, 1984, p. 254).

The designers drew on the American Unified Sciences and Mathematics for Elementary Schools (USMES, 1976) definition of a real problem as one which:

- Had an immediate practical effect on students' lives
- Led to some improvement in the situation of students
- Had no known right solutions nor clear boundaries
- Required students to use their own ideas for solving the problem.

They added a fifth criterion:

- That the problem 'is "big" enough to require many phases of class activity for effective solution'.

Practical science project

This project involved the design, collection and analysis of data; it replaced the use of laboratory work. Students were sent a home kit of instruments to help carry out the project. Project topics ranged from the fungi of rabbit dung, buttercup distribution in mown and unmown fields, fauna of gravel pits, to lugworms on sandy beaches. Students were allocated specialist tutors on the basis of a brief outline of their topic area. The project was supposed to take 36 hours, but the average time spent was much longer.

Material

The project guide included sections on:

Choosing a project
Suggested types of project
Publications which may be of help
Notes on using the home-based instruments
Statistics tests useful for analysis
Expected report format guidelines.

Many students received no face-to-face support as they were located some way from their specialist tutor. Telephone and correspondence tuition was provided; most contact was by letter.

Assessment

The project was assessed via a draft and final report. The first was graded by the course supervisor and the second by an independent tutor.

Technology design project

This project was part of a course concerned with the relationship between society, technology and design. It aimed to help students to explore, as much as provide ready answers. The project was almost completely open. It asked students to specify a problem situation, undertake an enquiry into that situation and specify what should be designed to solve the problem. The project was designed to take 60 hours (a third of the time allotted to the course); in fact the average time students spent on their projects was much longer. Students found the project demanding but virtually everyone (97 per cent) found it interesting (Cross and Ransome, 1977).

Materials

Project materials included a brief overview of what was required, assignment guidelines, plus three substantial items: a game designed to help students identify their project; a project guide which offered selection guidance and advice on project strategies, problems and pitfalls; and a design methods manual. This was a substantial collection of methods and techniques and students were expected to select from these and apply them in their project. Only half the students found the game helpful, whereas two thirds appreciated the other guidance supplied.

Assessment

The students were expected to submit two project assignments. The first one largely comprised the worksheets completed when playing the project identification game. It was to include a 500-word statement about one project. The second, some six months later, was a 2,000-word project report. Students were also expected to present a log of project-related activities together with any other material the student considered necessary.

Assessment criteria indicated two-thirds of the grade would be awarded for the way the project had been tackled and one-third for the project specification. The course also included an exam question on the project along the lines of: 'Describe and discuss methods you found useful in your project'.

Project-based practical arts course

The art and environment course is an example of how far one can go in offering freedom in the curriculum in open and distance learning situations. It centred on a practical arts course offered at a distance. Through this process, many students developed greater sensitivity to the environment and a sense of personal empowerment as a result of undertaking the course.

Materials

The support materials included a number of relatively short workbooks, TV and radio programmes designed to introduce the projects and above all stimulate the student.

The week-long residential component that supported 200 hours of distance study was a critical factor. This was held fairly early on in the course. Students picked their own tutor and many staff were fairly non-directive, though encouraging students to try new approaches. Many students started the week confused, even antagonistic to the course, but most left converted and went on to complete the remaining assignments eagerly.

Assessment

The main focus of the course was a series of projects, from which the student selected one or more for each of the five assignments.

The projects ranged from traditional artistic activity such as doing a self-portrait, through appreciation of the senses such as listening to silence or composing a score for different textured paper, to perceptual challenges such as enumerating one's own and partner's activities and categorizing these (typically a very revealing exercise), to more reflective projects like writing one's autobiography or challenges like doing something one had never done before.

Students were asked to send in notes explaining the rationale for their projects and how they went about them, in addition to the end product (Henry, 1987).

Technology project credit

The whole of this course is a project of the students' own choosing. Students are sent general advice, and expected to send in an outline of their proposed area. Topics have varied widely. Many students opt to do a project in an area in which they have considerable knowledge.

Tuition

Students are matched to a tutor on the basis of their initial outline. Where no suitable tutor is available, the student is not able to register for the course.

Tutors are expected to offer at least three two-hour tutorials apart from the initial pre-course meeting; two subsequent meetings are also suggested.

Assignments

There are three assignments plus an oral exam. The initial report accounts for 10 per cent of the marks, the interim report for 20 per cent, the final report 50 per cent and the oral the remaining 20 per cent of the grade awarded. The final report is marked by both the tutor and another examiner and these two both attend the oral exam.

As shown in Figure 2.2, the timing of the cut-off dates for each of these assignments helps student pace their work (Spear, 1977, offers a review).

Work-based project

Hotel and catering industry supervisors wishing to obtain a National Examining Board for Supervisory Management (NEBSM) certificate in supervisory management are required to undertake successfully a work-based project. The project aims to integrate learning and show students are able to apply this

Months	Student	Assignment	Tutorial	Comment
Sept/Oct		Student starts work		
Nov	Student and tutor meet		Initial tutorial	
Jan	Preliminary literature search		Possible tutorial	
Feb	Write initial report			
March		Initial report 15 March		
April			Tutorial	2 weeks later
May			Tutorial	One four-hour or two two-hour tutorials
June	Write interim report, including one complete section			
July		Interim report due 15 July		Tutorial
Aug	Write final report			
Sept		Final report due 15 September		Copies to tutor plus examiner
Oct		Oral exam		

Figure 2.2 *ODL project credit schedule*

knowledge. Students are asked to pick a practical problem at work that needs tackling and involves supervisory management, especially human resource and financial aspects. They are encouraged to pick an area they are personally committed to and that will benefit their work as well as themselves. During the project, students are expected to demonstrate their ability to: plan and organize and carry through a task; solve a problem; use initiative, imagination and originality; collect facts and evidence; analyse; think logically and communicate. Students are also encouraged to use a log allocating activities to particular weeks and keep a learning diary documenting their thoughts on the success or failure of the approaches they took, any changes in their style, others' reactions and future plans. The student has a work-based manager and a college-based tutor for advice and to assess their work.

Assessment
Students have to submit a project proposal and final report. Fairly detailed suggestions are provided as to the appropriate areas to cover in both the project

proposal and final report. For example, the proposal must include information on the background to the problem, its aims and objectives, the plan to meet these objectives, resources needed, obstacles anticipated, proposed time-scale and a discussion of how the project meets the student's development needs. Students are expected to discuss this project proposal with their manager and send it to their tutor. Interestingly, guidelines to the student's manager encourage him or her to give the student the same kind of support they would give an external consultant, including a discussion on problem identification, agreeing the plan, enabling access, lending authority to the task but also holding the student to the agreed deadlines and providing feedback. The 3,000-word project report is submitted to the student's manager and tutor. Assessment criteria include the quality of the report, its structure, the project's significance, appropriate methodology, ability to gather and use evidence, synthesize and draw conclusions, frame recommendations, construct an action plan, and reference course material (Hotel and Catering Training Company, 1993).

Group project exercise

Group projects are hard to offer in ODL if students are geographically dispersed. One strategy is to offer a group project during any phase where students do come together. For example, the OU introduction to psychology and cognitive psychology courses use the week-long residential school for this purpose. In-service training may present similar opportunities. Sunderland and Toncheva (1991) argue for the merits of using projects for INSET. Apart from being an excellent motivator and efficient way of teaching, projects, they point out, are particularly well suited to handling a wide range of participants' needs, abilities and interests within a single course.

Project work is becoming increasingly common in teaching English as a Foreign Language (EFL). Kennedy (1982) describes how group projects are used as the basis for a Master's degree in applied linguistics. Students are post-experience teachers of EFL, the course is designed to increase motivation and participation of students in the learning process. Staff considered a group project a more effective teaching methodology and expected it to produce greater content mastery. This process-orientated approach is also consistent with curriculum theory in EFL teaching.

Groups of students were asked to prepare a presentation to the whole class. The process involved nine steps:

1 The teacher gave a list of topics, each supported by three or four recommended readings plus a key question to address.
2 Course participants signed up for one topic.

3 Each group addressed a different topic and was given relevant reading for that topic.
4 The group chairperson distributed these and arranged for the group to meet.
5 Participants read the readings.
6 The group met to discuss the readings and how to present their essence.
7 The group members met with the lecturer to discuss what they had read, their presentation plan and any problems they wanted resolved.
8 The group prepared the class presentation.
9 The group presented its findings to the whole class.

Students showed considerable anxiety at the outset but were judged more confident in their exam performance.

Group projects may seem risky as different individuals may contribute different amounts to the project. However, the use of group-based projects is a much better reflection of the kind of team-based project that is the mainstay of many working environments. Helms and Haynes (1990) argue that even dysfuntional groups with a lot of conflict who are finding it hard to be cooperative offer an excellent learning environment and provide a better match to the real-world organizational environment. They argue that such groups offer the student the chance to learn to achieve a goal despite difficult individuals, to use multiple sources of information if one is controlled by someone unreliable, learn of the need for monitoring and tricks like allocating more than one person to a job if someone is not pulling their weight. Much conventional MBA teaching is also based on a form of group-based project known as the case study method. A group of students are set the task of reporting on a particular organization. Typically the group is under such time pressure that they have to split the load and rely on group members of varying ability. Finding ways of dealing with this to greatest effect is supposed to mirror later working life.

Independent study project

Some institutions adopt a problem-based approach where all teaching takes place through extended projects. For example, the School for Independent Study at the University of East London ran a two-year programme offering a Dip. HE by independent study. A third year was available for those wishing to convert this qualification to a degree.

Stephenson (1983) describes how the student is required to formulate his or her educational problem, seek a solution for it and demonstrate the extent to which he or she has been successful. The student is expected to make this explicit to college staff, through an interim and final statement. The process by which this is achieved can be split into three main parts:

- Interim statement
  a The student's educational experience
  b Their present position (their strengths and weaknesses)
  c Their future plans (after obtaining the diploma/degree)
- Programme plan
  d Skills, knowledge and qualities needed to complete the programme of independent study
  e Proposed programme of study (methods, objectives, areas of study, assignments to be completed)
- Final statement
  f Methods of assessment.

Parts a to c are written in sequence at the outset, over a period of a month or six weeks. Once the interim plan is accepted the student goes on to plan his or her programme of study. Discussions with a tutor are normally critical here. This plan, together with the proposed methods of assessment, are submitted as a final statement; this acts as a learning contract between the student and institution as to the nature of the student's proposed learning activities.

Assessment

The assessment products are expected to meet the objectives set out in d. Once the student has completed his or her programme, they submit the agreed assessment products to one external and two internal assessors.

School project

Katz and Chard (1992) give an example of a project for schoolchildren around the topic 'Water in our homes', a typically interdisciplinary topic. 'The children help determine the data to be collected; for example, where the water comes from, how it is treated, stored and pumped to the building their home is in, where it enters and leaves the home, its uses, quantities required for each use, its properties at different temperatures, the permeability of materials for roofing, clothing, etc. The children identify sub-topics of interest to them and select particular types of task they will be responsible for and the level of difficulty they engage in ... the feelings of mastery resulting from such sustained effort can lay the foundation for a life-long disposition to reach for an in-depth understanding'.

Katz and Chard suggest there are three main stages in the schoolchild's project:

1 Getting started, where children share their personal experiences and knowledge about the topic.

2 Project in progress, where children formulate questions about the topic they would like answered and investigate via a field trip interviewing local 'experts'.
3 Concluding the project involves presenting their findings through a play, visual displays and written work.

Review

All disciplines use project work. Projects may be thought of in four major groupings: the literature review, the information search, empirical research and design projects. Literature reviews are particularly commonplace in the humanities. Empirical projects can be subdivided into surveys, case studies and experiments. Surveys are common in the social sciences, case studies in education and management, experiments in science, design projects in technology, and simulations in mathematics and computing.

There have been successful open and distance learning courses which include project work as part of a course, or base all their assignments round projects, or where the entire course comprises a project. Where students are geographically separated, group projects are often reserved for times when students come together, eg at a residential meeting. Work-based projects often use a work-based mentor as adviser and sometimes also as assessor in addition to a college-based tutor.

Points for reflection

Which departments in your organization offer projects?
At what level?
Are there any departments which you feel would benefit from introducing projects?
Where would you like to offer projects?
Have you any ideas for group projects?

Chapter 3

History and appeal

> We might put vocation and intention back into the process of education, much more firmly than we had it there before (Bruner, 1971).

This chapter examines the history of project work in education and training and the reasons given for using this approach.

History

Projects revolve round problem-based investigation and since people have always had to solve problems, projects have been around a long time.

Adderley *et al.* (1975) give some examples of projects quoted by Swift (1726). In *Gulliver's Travels*, he is invited to visit the Academy of Projectors and describes the various projects underway, from 'extracting sunbeams from cucumbers, which were put into vials … and let out to warm the air in raw inclement summers', to extracting food from human excrement by 'removing the tincture it receives in the gall, making the odour exhale and scrumming off the saliva'. Science projects cited by Swift included 'a new method of building houses beginning at the roof and working downwards to the foundations'. There is also an arts project for improving speculative knowledge by mechanical operations, namely inscribing all words of a given language on wooden blocks on spindles that were then turned and the resulting (nonsense) combinations diligently transcribed by students for the benefit of humanity. As a parody of some of the projects I was asked to undertake as an undergraduate, Swift's satire is all too close for comfort! I trust my experience is no longer typical of educational projects generally.

The scholarly research typical of research students undertaking higher degrees represents a form of extended project that has been in common use for several centuries. However, use of the project approach further down the curriculum seems to be of more recent origin.

Pragmatism

Problem-based and project-based learning are associated with pragmatism, a philosophy stressing the merits of learning from the real world and concrete things rather than abstractions. The merits of direct experience and offering the student some measure of control over the learning experience are values that have come to be associated with 'progressive education', a movement which has helped popularize the use of project work in teaching and which drew heavily on the famous educationalist and philosopher John Dewey's philosophy.

Dewey was one of the project approach's earliest champions. In his text, *Democracy and Education* (1916) Dewey deplores the artificiality of education that stresses passivity through rote learning and 'finding out what the teacher wants'. He advocates instead the active approach of the problem-based method where students undertake a staged enquiry process, derived from science, involving problem identification, hypothesis formulation and the selection and application of the preferred solution. Dewey stressed that the problems tackled should be those that presented themselves to the student in the course of learning, not ones imposed by the teacher. Dewey also favoured the collaborative possibilities of group projects.

In vocational training

Adderley *et al.* (1975) trace use of the project method back to America at the turn of the century. Massachusetts vocational schools used the term to describe home projects where students had to apply what they had learnt at school to the home, farm or garden.

In an important essay, Kilpatrick (1918) argued the case for the project method, likening traditional methods of education to slavery on the grounds that the student's will is normally harnessed to that of the teacher. Like Dewey, he felt educational practice should reflect democratic values and a system which granted students more liberty of action and thought. Dewey argued very similar virtues for the problem method, arguing that students must be allowed the freedom to develop their will through educational experience rather than experience an educational process that represses them.

Kilpatrick went on to offer a four-fold classification of projects, subsuming Dewey's problem method under his third category:

Act	to embody some idea or plan in external form
Experience	to enjoy some aesthetic experience
Solve a problem	to solve a problem
Train	to obtain some degree of skill.

Kilpatrick saw the project as 'a hearty purposeful act' and recommended that 'we think of a project as a pro-ject something pro-jected'. Like Dewey, Kilpatrick was essentially a developmentalist, an educator who stressed the importance of a child-centred approach that took account of the learners' preferences. He believed that encouraging children to follow their interests would increase their capacity for self-direction and consciously-sought meaning, a necessary skill in an age of rapid change.

Sexton (1990) compares Kilpatrick's idea of 'the project method' with more recent ideas of the learning project – the means by which adults undertake informal learning (Tough, 1985). Sexton points out that both emphasize the learner's intention or purpose and the enquiry process through which learning takes place.

In schools

By the 1930s, projects were beginning to be more commonplace in the UK, and in the USA projects were championed as a common form of active learning. Gull (1933) speaks of projects as a natural method of education connecting students with the real world outside education's ivory tower.

The project method was conceived for and has been applied extensively in the teaching of children. For example, the use of project work is commonplace in primary schools, a trend aided in Europe by the influence of Montessori's ideas, and one which ties in with Piaget's influential views of cognitive development. This perspective views knowledge as emerging from an interaction with the physical and social environment. (This may be contrasted with behaviourism where the machine metaphor emphasizes shaping behaviour through repetition and reward.) The project approach allowed children to develop in their own unique way, to interact actively with others and have hands on experience of the physical world, allowing learning to emerge from an integration of cognitive and social experience (Kohlberg and Mayer, 1972.)

Projects were central to infant education in the UK in the Plowden period (the late 1960s and 1970s). It is perhaps surprising that projects caught on for the education of young children as they have obvious advantages for teaching adults and in higher education. Adderley *et al.* (1975) list several:

> The adult is better placed to deal with the autonomy offered in projects.
> Projects approximate to the research used in higher education and act as a preparation.
> Projects provide a model of self-education that can sustain an adult in the world of work.

In the 1950s and 60s, projects moved upwards into the secondary school with the Nuffield Science Project's advocacy of 'discovery-based learning'. Bruner's (1971) ideas on the importance of discovery-based learning stressed the importance of the child being actively involved in learning, selecting and transforming information and engaging in a process of construing, testing and re-construing as opposed to passively receiving information and memorizing it. He suggests that this kind of discovery-based learning is intrinsically motivating. He also points out that material of interest to the individual and organized by him or her in line with his or her own ways of thinking is more likely to be remembered. Morgan (1980) points out that discovery-based approaches focus more on finding out about the unknown rather than concentrating on the known.

Higher education

In the 1970s and 80s, the pressures to offer a more relevant curriculum, and perhaps also a need to offer students more autonomy in their learning, finally reached the mass of higher education. It is now almost universal for third-year undergraduates to be expected to undertake a major project. Many departments also make use of more limited projects in the earlier years, partly as a means of preparing students for what is to come. A survey by Chambers (1964; 1972) of the use of project work in the final year of study in UK undergraduate science departments showed an increase from 14 to 67 per cent between 1964 and 1970. In the USA in the early 1970s, Dressel and Thompson (1973, p.19) claimed that the use of project work was pre-eminent in independent study. They write that it was the most commonly used form of independent study in three-quarters of the liberal arts colleges and universities surveyed.

We have also seen the rise of the group project at most levels of the curriculum. Group projects may be undertaken collectively, but are still usually reported separately by each individual involved, especially higher up the curriculum in further and higher education and where the report counts for assessment. Some professional training offers assessment of the group and a few brave souls have experimented with peer assessment.

The humanistic philosophy current in the late 1960s and 70s provided further impetus to the more radical use of project work in independent study and problem-based learning, where the student is responsible for determining the content of the whole curriculum. For example, Rogers (1969) argued that 'significant learning takes place when the subject matter is perceived as having relevance for [the learner's] own purposes'. This comes about when the student 'chooses his own direction, helps to discover his own learning resources, formulates his own problems and decides his own course of action and lives with the consequences of each of these choices', a form of experiential learning that develops the learner.

A number of writers in the 1970s and 80s have emphasized the importance of developing the student's autonomy, capacity for self-direction and independent study (see, for example, Boud, 1981; Knowles, 1975). In the last 15 years various initiatives concerned with the industrial relevance of education, such as the Training and Vocational Education Initiative Review and the Royal Society of Arts Education for Capability movement, have stimulated the use of project work further.

In today's ever-changing world, with instantaneous database access to well-structured knowledge, many educators also argue that the transferable 'learning to learn skills' fostered in project work are more useful than subject knowledge. For example, the School for Independent Study of the University of East London prospectus (1975) stated:

> We in the School for Independent Study hold that in our modern society much knowledge becomes obsolete. We therefore believe that it is more important to possess the ability to adapt to a new situation and to acquire new information than it is to retain knowledge in particular subjects .... The function of the school is to help people define their intellectual and social needs .... This is done by a 'problem-centred approach' to learning – that is by encouraging students ... to formulate problems, propose solutions and then put them into practice to test them.

Even if they are unwilling to go this far, many educators have sympathy with the idea of making education more relevant and find project work an obvious and acceptable route through which to offer socially relevant and useful activities.

Open learning

One of the current major changes in teaching methods is the rapid increase in open learning. Initially, individualized study at a distance was correspondence-based and students were presented with little more than book lists and a string of essay questions. The 1950s and 60s saw the rise of programmed learning where all the knowledge to be learnt was carefully structured down to the last detail. This approach was superseded by distance education, where teachers assimilated the material to be learnt and presented specially written texts in an educationally user-friendly format. The snag was that by so doing they had, in some ways, done the learning for the student.

It was originally thought to be impractical to offer project work at a distance but gradually staff have become more adventurous and we now see an increase in the amount of project work on offer in ODL institutions. In fact, one in nine of the course descriptions in the International Centre for Distance Learning database includes the term 'project' or 'project work'. One might expect that it would be difficult to offer much project work in a distance teaching institution as it is traditionally expected to require extra supervision, a luxury distance learning can rarely afford, but as we shall see in chapters to come there are ways of anticipating and preparing the students for problems they often raise with supervisors and cutting back on the amount of supervision time traditionally required.

Training

The use of project-based learning in training is also now widespread. The rapid expansion of open learning and partnership-based training (whereby staff can be trained and accredited without having to leave work) often increases the role for projects. Such schemes often revolve around the use of modular-based open learning units and project work. The projects provide an opportunity for the student to apply the course material to their working environment. These projects are often based in the student's own organization and address real problems the student is facing. It is increasingly common for such projects to be jointly supervised by an in-company mentor and college-based tutor.

Why offer projects?

This section offers some of the reasons given for teaching through projects. Studies at the Open University asking staff to volunteer their reasons for doing so, suggest there are five major reasons for using projects in open and distance learning: first, to ensure students are able to *apply their knowledge*; second, to *teach higher cognitive skills*; and third, to *motivate* students by offering activities of greater relevance to them. The remaining two centre upon advocacy of projects as an *assessment*-sorting device and a means of offering students greater *autonomy*. Many academics argue that stretching the student via a project is a necessary part of a rounded and demanding assessment process. More radical educators feel it is incumbent upon educators to teach via a process which gives learners more control of the learning process and takes much greater account of their interests. Another reason for using projects is that they often provide very good *preparation for working life* (Henry, 1978a; 1984). Cornwall (1975) presents a similar picture. He asked his science and technology colleagues to rate in order of importance a fairly comprehensive list of reasons for offering project work. The three most common reasons cited were: to provide an additional means of assessment; to stimulate individual initiative; and to provide training in the methods of the relevant profession. Figure 3 summarizes the main reasons for teaching through projects. These will be discussed in turn.

Application of knowledge	• Learn to apply knowledge
	• Understand a discipline better
Preparation for work	• Necessary technical training
	• Provide professional practice
Teaching cognitive skills	• Teach higher cognitive skills
	• Avoid spoonfeeding
Assessment	• Sorts sheep from goats
	• Necessary standard
Motivation	• Motivating
	• More effective
Relevance	• Offers autonomy
	• Fosters responsibility

Figure 3.1 *Reasons for offering project work*

Application of Knowledge

> So much we do is very abstract, projects make it real (ODL undergraduate project student).

Perhaps the most common reason for including project work in the curriculum is to enable the learner to apply the knowledge they have learned. So it is no accident that the use of project work is particularly common in applied disciplines such as research, management, agriculture, nursing, engineering, environment, design and architecture. I found that it was also common in subjects with an obviously interdisciplinary nature such as psychology, systems and biology (Henry, 1978a).

Projects are usually designed to teach discipline-specific skills and/or general transferable academic skills. The OU study found that most of the academics who have included a project in their course felt they were necessary for students to obtain an adequate grasp of the subject. Academics, tutors and students argued that the general transferable academic skills fostered by projects were necessary to enable students to apply what they have learnt.

The ability to apply knowledge is a very different skill from merely understanding theory in the abstract. For example, I have taught statistics students who were perfectly able to pass an exam asking about statistics, but who were unable to apply that knowledge to the rather more messy and imprecise world of live data. Hence academics teaching research methods felt it was insufficient for students to merely reproduce the principles of good research; rather they had to learn how to apply these principles to new research problems. They also needed to be able to follow arguments in research articles and be in a position to come to some conclusion as to their validity. Thus students needed to be equipped with the practical skills to do research and the evaluative skills necessary to assess literature critically. Projects provide the obvious route to teach such skills.

Understand a discipline

A very similar point applies in pure disciplines. Historians often feel it is essential for students to deal with primary source material first-hand and social scientists feel that students need to carry out some research themselves to get a real understanding of the discipline and its methodology. Likewise, scientists feel students should have to design and conduct their own experiments. In all these disciplines project work enables the student to get a feel for the procedures used to derive knowledge in the discipline and perhaps more particularly the tenuousness of some of the data on which it is based.

Preparation for work

Technical training

In technical subjects some form of project may be the only way to provide the necessary training, as competency in the subject being taught involves an ability to carry out some process, whether this be architecture, engineering or building. Design technologists, for example, feel students must carry out projects to develop a proper understanding of the processes involved. Gault and Synder (1978) argue that by the final year, engineering students worry that they will not be able to apply their knowledge in the real world and that design projects provide the ideal way of training the students in the skills that will be expected of them. Thus the project does not just teach students how to apply skills but actually prepares them very directly for the world of work.

Some authors (for example, Riley, 1980; Sims, 1976) point out that much of the student's subsequent working life is likely to be spent undertaking teamwork, be they engineers, managers or in the caring professions. As a consequence these writers champion the merits of *group projects* as a better preparation for real life and argue that such experiences ought to be included in the further and higher education curriculum, not just in schools.

Professional training

Traditionally a thesis or dissertation is the key element in a Masters degree programme. Here the student is expected to undertake traditional scholarly research. With the advent of professional Masters degrees such as the MBA (Masters in Business Administration), or in the US Master of Advertising, etc. the traditional thesis may be less relevant. For example, Singletary and Crook (1986) point out that the skills and methods required by traditional theses are often not the ones that contribute most to the professional needs of a Masters in Journalism. They report a trend to replace the traditional thesis with a professional project; this might mean carrying out an investigative report, library research or a film and video presentation. The traditional thesis is more likely to involve conducting historical research, a survey or content analysis; areas where students often lack the necessary training in historiography, quantitative methods, etc. and the inclination to master them, since such competences are not relevant to their future professional practice. They also report the typical 5–6,000-word project was given less time and weighting in the programme than the traditional thesis.

In professional subjects like business there is a body of thought that suggests a much greater portion of business education should take place in the organizational environment. The argument is that worthwhile learning occurs through personal involvement with management issues on the ground as they happen, and that analysing cases reporting on such situations after the event is no substitute. Work on the domain-specific character of problem finding and solving skills provides support for this position (see, for example, Kauffmann, 1991; Mangham, 1986). Projects provide an ideal educational vehicle for offering and assessing learning in 'real' environments. In MBA assignments, students may be asked to implement and evaluate some part of a real task; here the project simulates parts of a manager's job in a very real sense.

Higher cognitive skills

> ... being able to express yourself is a key part. A project forces the student to do the research, think out the rationale of their research project and explain it clearly so anyone can understand it.　　　　(ODL project tutor)

A related reason for offering projects is to present students with a task that develops the higher cognitive skills of organizing, synthesizing, analysing and evaluating. The traditional essay often asks a student to do little more than regurgitate pre-existing material. ODL assignments which expect the student to refer to no more than the units of material they have been sent may help students pick out key points, write clearly, succinctly and logically, but do little to develop or test the students' other cognitive abilities. In a project, a student not only collects material but has to organize, analyse, synthesize and evaluate it. The nature of the task forces him or her to think things out for themself, so stimulating cognitive skills. Kennedy (1982) also advocates the use of projects as a particularly good method of drawing out each individual's existing experience and expertise.

Projects foster a number of general competencies including:

- self-direction – the capacity to carry out a competent piece of work independently; a skill that takes initiative
- inventiveness – the creative use of resources, alternative methods and explanations
- problem-solving abilities – a diagnostic ability, problem formulation, problem solving, analytical and evaluative skills
- integrative skills – the synthesis of ideas, experience and information from different sources and disciplines
- decision-making skills – deciding what is relevant and what is not, what to include and what to leave out
- interpersonal communication skills – communicating with individuals and elucidating ideas through the written word.

It has been argued that self-direction, problem-solving, decision-making and communication skills applied to real problems are transferable and provide a better preparation for personal and professional life than more traditional methods of teaching.

The project approach emphasizes action and the process of induction. Gorb (1987) argues that this is a necessary counterbalance to traditional education's emphasis on reflection, analysis and deduction – traditions associated with science and scholasticism. Gorb points out the superiority of the project approach over the case method in training students for action; projects require the student to synthesize, work with others and implement and thus offer practice in getting things done whereas the former – where groups of students study a succession of real cases – is essentially focused round analytic enquiry and communicative skills in articulating analysis.

Avoid spoonfeeding

> Usually when we produce students we do the learning for them, scholarly inventiveness occurs during the process of finding material and making connections and all our students get fed is the results.
> (ODL course developer)

The use of project work also helps counteract any criticism that teachers are doing the 'learning' for the student by spoonfeeding them with neatly packaged dollops of ready organized knowledge. As a means of conveying information, lectures have long been discredited and open learning modules are increasingly becoming the norm as the way to convey knowledge. However the use of these perfectly designed pre-digested units of learning material leaves open and distance learning particularly vulnerable to the charge of spoonfeeding students. Project work provides the perfect counter to stretch the student, make them apply knowledge and take initiative. ODL staff also sometimes feel that projects help maintain academic standards by countering the claim of spoonfeeding.

Open learning can combine the best of both worlds by using distance education learning modules with locally supervised project work so students can study with sufficient written back-up to allow a depth of knowledge and its application in areas of their own choosing. As the library of ODL modules develops, students will find increasing ease in accessing relevant modules for their particular project.

Assessment

Many people argue that projects are a necessary part of assessment, as they provide a more demanding test of ability than either the traditional three-hour exam or essays on pre-specified sources.

Sorts sheep from goats

By placing much more responsibility for decisions and learning with the student, project work is more demanding than more traditional schooling where the student typically plays a more passive role. The demanding nature of projects leads some teachers to argue they are valuable as a means of sorting out the sheep from the goats. Some studies of project assessment have shown a tendency towards a bi-modal distribution of marks, perhaps supporting the contention that project work is indeed a good discriminator.

Necessary standard for higher level, professional and applied courses

Many staff and students feel a sizeable project should be a compulsory element in most higher level, professional and applied courses, especially an undergraduate degree. Others feel the requirement for a compulsory project credit should be restricted to honours degrees. This argument is also applied to ODL courses; for example, over half the students in the OU study felt a course with a sizeable project should be compulsory for an OU honours or general degree. (Experience seemed to affect attitude here, as students doing structured projects were pretty evenly split as to whether or not this was desirable, but on the unstructured projects there was a clear majority in favour of a compulsory project.)

Basically the argument is not so much on the grounds that projects offer an enjoyable or valuable experience, but that projects are necessary to ensure students learn how to, and can demonstrate their ability to, undertake an independent enquiry process. Students and staff recognize that projects teach important skills which can not be acquired in any other way, or not easily so. They recognize that projects are often very demanding but feel that the responsibility placed on students in the design of a project, location of material, analysis and organization, and the necessary use of initiative and problem-solving skills, are a better test of ability than ordinary course work. In addition, open learning students sometimes have the notion that since students in other universities do projects, they should too.

Motivation and effectiveness

More effective method of teaching

Many teachers advocate the use of projects simply because they believe them to be a more effective form of teaching. For example, many language teachers believe teaching from text is an inefficient way to learn a language. They advocate an approach involving a series of mini-projects, where students attempt to speak the foreign language while undertaking common activities such as making a meal, going to the library, etc. (see, for example, Hilton-Jones, 1988; Koeller 1984). Much the same argument is put forward by teachers in many other disciplines. For example, Litogoy (1991) argues the case for mini-projects to teach history: 'Student involvement and responsibility develop thinking and result in greater learning achievement'.

In institutions with a limited course profile, a project course has the advantage of allowing students more choice by enabling them to follow their own interests without the organization having to produce additional material.

Soft experientialists' motivation

Other people use projects because they believe them to be more motivating to students. For example, Gibbons (1984) advocates 'challenge education' which asks students to carry out projects in five areas: a practical skill, logical enquiry process, creative expression, some kind of voluntary service and something that is an adventure. This type of approach encourages the learner to start thinking in terms of what they can do.

Many educators recognize that students learn better when they have some control over the learning process. Various studies (for example, Brennen and Percy, 1977; Penland, 1977; Tough, 1985) have shown that the part of their studies that learners find most beneficial are those where they feel stimulated and challenged and have some freedom to determine the content and approach. Project work is a prime example of a teaching method that offers these advantages. Considerable evidence suggests students do indeed tend to become very involved with projects where they have had some say in the topic studied, often putting in many hours over and above those demanded. Students who have some kind of control over planning their learning are also more likely to reflect on what they need, discover how to tailor approaches to suit them and get the satisfaction that comes from initiating, planning and seeing through a project, as well as retaining better what they have learnt.

Projects have a special role in open learning institutions such as the Open University for two other reasons. Mature students are better placed to profit from project work than their adolescent counterparts at traditional universities in that they have already developed strong interests in certain areas (eg, local history) or have come across problems at work that they would like to follow up in more depth. This conjecture is supported by the OU finding that the three most significant factors in deciding on a project were 'interest in subject', 'knew something about subject' and 'tied in with my work'.

Relevance, control and autonomy

The project method also affords an opportunity to offer tasks that are more relevant to the student since he or she is granted control over the subject matter and approach.

Hard experientialists
Staff motivation for including project work in the curriculum varies. For example, there are those I have termed the 'soft experientialists', who use experiential methods such as project work because they believe them to be more motivating and effective, and the 'hard experientialists' who employ such an approach due to a more radical educational philosophy (Henry, 1992). The hard experientialist believes that education should use methods that offer the student

autonomy in learning, give them control over the process and the opportunity to pick topics of relevance to them (see, for example, Boud, 1989). Problem-based learning and the project-oriented universities are practical embodiments of this kind of approach. Problem-based learning can be thought of as teaching subjects almost entirely through project work; it has a particular appeal in applied disciplines such as agriculture (see, for example, Packham *et al.*, 1989) and medicine. Similarly, several European universities such as the University of Vincennes and University of Aalborg have attempted to base the entire curriculum around project work.

To summarize, the hard experientialists' reasons for offering project work include the following:

- relevance – some argue that what is learnt is more *relevant* to the task eventually performed, (eg, doctors learn more about common presenting problems and less about Latin names of the smallest bones in the body)
- intrinsic motivation – some argue, with Montessori teachers, that allowing the child to choose what and when they want to learn will avoid squashing their natural inclinations and is more likely to produce a *self-motivated* healthy adult
- autonomy – others argue that the methods used should reflect the desired end, ie, an *autonomous* interested learner who knows how to learn and communicate
- metacompetences – given databases with their 'knowledge on tap', the skills of problem solving, *learning to learn*, decision making and communication cultivated through projects are more relevant to today's needs
- learner management – radicals believe that it if we are to create a society of responsible individuals able to use initiative appropriately, sensitively and efficiently we must teach them via a process that gives them *control* of the learning process so they are able to develop their initiative skilfully. This amounts to a radically different philosophy from that underlying didactic teaching.

Drawbacks

Along with these advantages, project work has a cost, notably the extra demands it tends to make on the curriculum, staff and students. Some drawbacks of projects are that they:

- demand a lot of the student
- take a long time
- need extra supervision
- need careful design to work well

- benefit from preparatory training exercises
- can involve extra expense
- are supposedly difficult to assess
- are time-consuming to assess.

Demanding

Projects are more demanding than the average essay and place much more responsibility on the student. Certain students thrive on the freedom they are offered; others wallow and prefer the surer ground of a predetermined topic, methodology and content.

Time

A project needs to be allocated a fairly generous amount of time if it is to be substantial enough to offer a student some real payback. The student needs to go beyond merely collecting material and needs sufficient time to ponder, organize, analyse and synthesize material. Projects are also relatively demanding on teaching time.

This time has to be found at the expense of covering less material elsewhere in the curriculum. For example, the OU's research methods course offered students 29 instead of the usual 32 units of course material to allow extra study time to complete the project work in the course. Staff often find it hard to decide which material they are prepared to drop.

Restricted scope

Most student projects are necessarily fairly restricted in scope. This can be problematic in certain areas. For example, in undertaking quantitative research, students need a fairly substantial database, probably one that is too large for them to collect themselves, before they can undertake any sensible analysis. This problem needs careful design. It would be possible, for instance, to get a group of students to collect data and share them, or to separate data collection and analysis projects and use pre-existing data for the analysis.

Training

Ideally students undertaking projects should be trained in the skills they will need to undertake the task. Often the philosophy applied is that of 'sink or swim', and remarkably little preparatory training is given.

Expense

Another drawback of projects for the impecunious is that they can involve students in considerable expense, in travelling to and from the sites, such as libraries, companies or old churches, and in acquiring appropriate source material and paying for documents, photos, etc.

Assessment

Many people perceive the major drawback of project work as the difficulty of assessing assignments fairly. While projects do take longer to mark than conventional assignments, staff often find them more interesting and I have some evidence to suggest the reliability is no worse than essays (see Chapter 9).

Review

It is probably true that most courses at all levels of study in schools, colleges and universities incorporate some form of project work. Project work was championed by Dewey, Kilpatrick and Montessori early this century. In the Plowden years it became commonplace in primary schools. Nuffield's advocacy of science projects helped the approach gain ground in secondary schools. It has been widely used in the final year of studies in higher education. Project learning was originally deemed to be difficult if not impossible to supervise at a distance but is now increasingly common in open learning. The approach is central to many of the new educational initiatives aimed at increasing access, competency and enterprise, such as National Vocational Qualifications (NVQs), Training and Enterprise Councils (TECS), and Enterprise in Higher Education (EHE).

Including project work in the curriculum has many advantages. It offers students a means of following their own interests and staff a means of motivating students while encouraging the development of higher cognitive skills and assessing the student's abilities at undertaking independent work; it also offsets the charge that ODL spoonfeeds students. Satisfactory projects generally need an extended time period, which tends to eat into the time available for other curriculum material. Projects involve additional supervisory and assessment duties, but reward staff and learners through inherently more interesting work.

Points for reflection

Does your institution offer more project work now than in the past?
Think back on the projects you have undertaken –
What were the reasons for including them in the curriculum?
What do you feel you and the students gained from doing them?
What were the drawbacks?

Section B: PROCESS

I'm not saying I didn't enjoy it, but it's certainly the most difficult task I've had to do in six years of studying.

Projects can be thought of as entailing three main stages of enquiry: deciding on a topic, collecting material, and analysing and writing up. It is the thesis of this book that the difficulties students experience with projects are related to the stage of the project. The OU study showed that more students experienced difficulty in analysing the data and writing the report than deciding on a topic or collecting information. The type of project is also important; for example, the majority of students on unstructured projects had difficulty at each stage, but on structured projects the majority only experienced difficulty analysing and writing up the project work (Henry, 1978a). In his research on individual learning projects, Tough (1967) found individuals typically experienced difficulty with about three tasks, including choosing a goal, planning the activities, and obtaining resources.

My research (Henry, 1978a, b, 1984, 1992) has led me to the conclusion that regardless of the type of project, each stage presents common pitfalls summarized in Figure B.1. Chapters 4 to 6 expand on these and suggest ways of addressing them.

Deciding
  Anxiety
  Overambition
  Interest versus feasibility

Collecting
  Underestimating workload
  Waiting time
  Side-tracking

Analysing and writing up
  Difficulty
  Over-involvement

Figure B.1 *Pitfalls associated with different stages of project work*

Chapter 4

Deciding on a topic

There were so many possibilities I just didn't know what to do.
(ODL project student)

Sometimes the project topic is set, sometimes students have to choose between a series of options and sometimes the choice is open-ended.

Deciding on a topic and formulating a proposal is a task students typically find more difficult than their teachers anticipate. The amount of difficulty experienced varies according to the student, but the OU project study showed that, on average, over half the students undertaking projects found it very or fairly difficult to decide on a topic for their project (Henry, 1978a).

Staff need to build in thinking time. For instance, the University of East London's School for Independent Study originally allocated six weeks for students to decide on a project for the year. Students found this insufficient and the period allocated was extended (Ramsden, 1977). In a wide range of unstructured projects, I found the decision stage took about 10 per cent of the total time the student spent on the project (Henry, 1978b; see Figure 7.2, Chapter 7).

Students usually welcome some help in deciding on a topic. In the OU project study, three-quarters of students found the advice given helpful and around two-fifths would have liked more assistance. Certain types of students seem to need this more than others. The OU study suggested nearer a half of the students would have welcomed extra assistance on courses where little guidance was given, the instructions were a little unclear or they had to decide between options. Even on courses where fairly full advice was given, around a third would have liked more help from their tutor. However, these figures declined to under a fifth where the written advice was particularly well structured, so it is possible to teach well-prepared projects at a distance without much support from a tutor.

Generally, students are given a free choice of project or set the same or related projects; however, some teachers have successfully mixed the two, allowing students a free choice or the opportunity of doing a set project. (Similarly picking your own area or tackling a problem in your supervisor's area are both acceptable routes to a Ph.D in most disciplines.) For example, the OU systems failures course provided a folder of materials as the basis for a project for those not wishing to choose their own. The set topic may seem to be the easier bet yet OU experience suggests many open learning students prefer to undertake a project in an area of their choice.

Another strategy is to offer a project that provides useful data year on year. For example, Fail (1991) describes an on-going project on seedling survivability, in which students can compare their data with that obtained in previous years.

Difficulties

- Finding an appropriate topic
- Having to change topics.

Appropriate topics

There is no doubt there is an art to selecting an appropriate project topic, and this is something one gets better at with experience, which is little comfort for the student new to project work.

Jankowicz (1991) advises his management project students to pick a topic they have worked on before, something they are good at and in an area in which they are comfortable.

Changing projects

Nearly a third of students in the OU study found they had to change projects part way through. The main reasons for changing projects were:

- difficulty obtaining information
- being too ambitious
- the initial choice was proving to be too time-consuming
- found more interesting alternative
- lack of information.

Difficulty in finding information was common on humanities projects using primary source material, social science projects using published data and field-based science projects. It was less problematic for projects involving interviews with people than for those relying on documents. Lack of data seemed to afflict humanities students in particular. Overambition necessitating a change in project affected more students on applied social science and design projects. Projects being too time-consuming leading to a topic change was particularly common on courses where all the assignments were projects-based or the course involved a number of mini-projects. Nearly half of the design project students changed projects because they found a more interesting alternative.

Hodgson and Murphy (1984) found a fifth of their distance education science students, doing one of four structured projects, ending up changing projects. Three of the options involved field work and one a computer simulation. One option concerned an investigation of the genetic polymorphism for colour in the two-spot ladybird. Alas, a lack of two-spot ladybirds in 1982 was the main reason that led a third of students choosing this project to change options!

Common pitfalls

Three problems are almost universal in the early stages of a project; these are:

- Anxiety
- Overambition
- Interest versus feasibility.

Anxiety

The project comes up first as a symbol of anxiety, an unknown quantity. Students are eager to discuss it without any tangible reference to an idea. Gradually as they approach the time when they have to think of ideas they become even more upset wondering whether these are feasible or possible! (Tutor)

Many students are apprehensive about the idea of doing a project at the outset. They may be unclear about what is expected of them. They may be nervous about their ability to undertake a large piece of work. Often learners find they are expected to undertake a fairly substantial project and little or nothing is provided by way of preparation for this experience. The OU study of students on 20 different project courses at advanced levels of study (Henry, 1978a) found two-fifths of students had never done any kind of project prior to the one they were currently undertaking.

However, this anxiety is not restricted to novices. Kennedy (1982) found her sample of experienced teachers were anxious about the prospect of group projects that only involved presenting findings orally to their peers. Sunderland and Toncheva (1991) also report anxiety about project work in a population of in-service teachers. The most commonly expressed reason for this anxiety was uncertainty about what to do.

Often the project element in a course is compulsory and the student is required to achieve a pass to be eligible for a course credit. This may enhance any feelings of anxiety.

Overambition

> You have to dissuade them from anything too grandiose.
> (Tutor)

> Students need frequent encouragement and advice on how to proceed with their work. I made a very concerted effort to be as flexible as possible about changes in plans and the inevitable cut-back in the scope of originally over-ambitious projects.
> (Fail, 1991)

Paradoxically, although frightened by the scope of the enterprise, the typical project student is chronically overambitious, often picking subjects worthy of a doctorate rather than, say, 50 or 100 hours work. Being unaware of the amount of work involved they may intend to research a whole industry, cover a wide span of history or pick something vague to investigate. This matters as students can waste time gathering data for an inappropriately large topic and find themselves overwhelmed with material.

The OU study found that in retrospect anything from 20 to 50 per cent of students doing unstructured projects felt they had been overambitious. Over a half had to narrow their original project topic and this figure rose to two-thirds on the larger unstructured projects. Around a quarter of the students who changed projects part way through claim that one of the main reasons they changed projects was an overambitious initial choice, and a similar number claim that the topic was too time-consuming.

This problem is not unique to projects; most researchers end up curtailing the scope of the research they envisaged at the outset (Philips, 1981). In an extended piece of research some slippage is allowed but a project is typically operating to a tighter schedule, so students need to be directed to an appropriate topic before they waste too much time investing their energies too widely.

Interest versus feasibility

> It is important to bear in mind the limited time when advising on projects; most students pick subjects out of interest, with little thought to the likely availability of sources.
> (Tutor)

Project work is one point in the curriculum where students have some scope for directing the content of their learning, so it is perhaps not surprising that the overwhelming factor in determining project choice is *interest* in the subject; a factor cited by over four-fifths of Open University students on project courses (Henry, 1978b).

This sounds laudable but, because time is limited, students are much better advised picking a topic where they are reasonably certain that suitable source material will be available. For example, the OU architecture project asked students to investigate the history of a building of their choice. The idea of investigating their own house appealed to many students but as private buildings are less well documented than public ones, the town hall is likely to be the safer bet.

On average only around a third of the OU students considered *feasibility* as a significant factor in their initial project topic choice. (Higher percentages applied to students on the larger project components and courses where all the assignments were project-based.)

Other factors that influence the students' choice of topic include *time*, which was mentioned by a quarter of the OU sample. Minimizing travel was also a significant factor for around half the students on projects involving site visits. Hodgson and Murph's (1984) biology students undertaking a relatively short structured project favoured science projects that could be carried out at home.

Knowing something about the *area* was mentioned by anything from a quarter to three-quarters of the OU students depending on the discipline. This factor tended to be more prominent in social science, education and technology projects but not the humanities.

On certain applied areas like public administration and teaching, half to two-thirds of students picked topics because they tied in with their *work*; indeed they were often encouraged to do so by the academics setting the project. This figure can be much higher for management projects. In design and systems courses a third were also able to pick a project that was relevant to their work.

Facilitative devices

Project designers can help students decide on an appropriate topic by:

- Materials
  - providing general advice
  - suggesting a topic list
  - offering sample reports
- Schedule
  - despatching materials early
  - appropriate decision timing
- Assessment
  - agreeing an outline plan
  - providing topic approval before work starts
- Tuition
  - giving an early tutorial
  - arranging field trips

Materials

General advice
The OU study found two-thirds of students felt general advice would have helped them decide.

The University of Surrey (1984) begins with the following general advice for their distance learning project in the Diploma in Higher Education:

> This is a piece of work which is very much your own. It could be a course design, the production of learning materials, a feasibility study, a theoretical report or even a small piece of research – just to list a few possibilities.

It goes on to offer teachers the following criteria to aid their project choice:

Is it workable?
  Do you have the necessary skills?
  Will you be able to obtain all the resources you need?
  Do you have adequate access to the people and situations you propose investigating?
  Can you complete the project in the time available?
Is it interesting ?
  Have you chosen a project with an outcome that interests you?
  Does it have practical implications?
  Who will benefit?

Katz and Chard (1992) suggest the following guidelines to help aid selection of a workable project for schoolchildren:

The topic:
    relates to everyday first-hand experience
    can be investigated in college rather than out
    allows an integration of subject or disciplines
    starts from real objects rather than abstract concepts
    will take at least a week to investigate
    allows problem solving and collaboration
    has good local resources.

General advice can also include some warnings on what to avoid. For example, half the Open University students studying unstructured projects felt a specific warning against the danger of being overambitious would have helped. This figure varied with the length of project: the longer the project the greater the need to forewarn.

Topic list

> You need more direction in the choice of a suitable project as it is too easy
> to attempt something too big, perhaps a checklist of topics.
> (ODL project student)

One strategy for providing the student with some indication of what is expected is to offer a list of project topics. Two-fifths of the OU project students wished they had been shown sample project topics. The reason that they were not all given the option is that some academics and teachers worry that this may defeat the purpose of the exercise of offering a project if students merely follow one of the indicative topics. In fact, I found only 6 per cent of students based their project topic on one suggested in the course material (Henry, 1989b).

However, it must be added that some students prefer this kind of concrete guidance. Blacklock (1975) found a fifth of her sample of ODL technology project students were attracted to the idea of choosing the project from a list, but three-quarters of her sample were not. (This sample was probably biased in favour of projects as three-quarters also favoured project to non-project courses.)

Sample projects

Another way of giving students a feel for what is required is to provide sample projects. They help students appreciate the intended scope, the level of detail required and the type of information that is important. Academics sometimes fear that providing such a model will lead to students copying the model suggested.

OU experience suggests that this fear is unfounded and that students go on to produce varied and creative work. However, OU students' motivation may be different from that of students in other sectors.

Scheduling

> You should start thinking about [your project] at an early stage of the course and discuss it with staff members who will advise you on it. You will not normally complete the project until towards the end of the course (University of Surrey, 1984).

Experience suggests that there is a strong case for alerting students to the fact that they will have to do a project as soon as possible, deferring the topic decision longer than the teacher expects, and warning them that everything will take longer than expected.

Despatch materials early

> It needs to be more clearly flagged in the early stages.
> (ODL project student)

> Plan the project much earlier in the course so that subsequent study through the material can be done with the needs of the project in mind.
> (ODL project student)

Students often get a better idea of what is expected as they learn more about the subject. In courses where the project is merely one component in a larger course, Open University experience suggests students would prefer to have all the course and project materials as early as possible to allow themselves familiarization and mulling-over time. This gives students a chance to educate themselves in the subject area and get a feel for what is required and what they might do. Three-quarters of Open University students on unstructured project courses wanted all the project material at the start of the course. This applied even where the project itself was not scheduled until some months later in the course. It helps to have skimmed relevant documents and to have the upcoming project as an idea in the back of your mind.

Decision timing

> I think you need some sort of preparatory thinking, not just come in at the beginning and start straight off.
> (ODL project student)

> I can't see how to do this, but move it earlier in the course.
> (ODL project student)

Another critical factor is the point at which the student is expected to decide on the project. Often a student is either expected to decide on a topic early on in a course so arrangements may be made for a suitable tutor to be allocated or it is left until the end where the project comprises the final part of the course. Open University experience suggest that students have a marked preference for being allowed to decide on a topic part way through the course, so they have had time to get a better feel for the material but have enough time left to collect material. For courses running over a nine-month period, we found months three to six provided the best starting point for project components.

A clear trend is evident between the date at which the student is asked to decide on their project topic and the month in which they were supposed to do so. Two-thirds of those asked to decide at the end of the course consider this too late and over a half of those asked to decide in the first month consider this too early. Similarly, about a third consider the the second month to soon and around a quarter found month seven too late. With one exception three-quarters are happy to decide in months three to six, ie, a third to two-thirds of the way through the course (Henry, 1978a).

Assessment

Outline and topic approval

> Get the elements completed and handed in as early as possible, especially an introduction and general outline.
> (ODL project student)

A brief project outline forces the student to start thinking about their project and allows the tutor to comment on its suitability. Experienced tutors emphasize the importance of firmly advising against anything they think will not work. Requiring the tutor to agree the project topic may also help curtail the overly-ambitious topics. (Chapter 9 elaborates on assessment procedures for project work.)

Tuition

Tutorial

> I didn't really understand what was wanted, someone should have made it clear.
> (ODL project student)

It would have been useful at the beginning if there had been a tutorial going through some of the problems one might encounter.
(ODL project student)

An early tutorial has a number of benefits. Students often find considerable relief from their anxieties just through realizing other students have similar concerns. The tutorial gives the tutor a chance to explain what is involved and divert students' generalized anxieties into more focused concerns on how to set about the task. Like me, Kennedy (1982) found a tutorial with the lecturer was a necessary means of reducing student anxiety about the task on her group projects.

Field trips
In some more specialist areas students may need field trips to give them ideas of the kind of thing that is possible. For example, the Open University ecology course offers an early field-based residential to give students experience of field skills. Fail (1991) describes how he took his students on a series of field trips to urban and natural ecosystems such as a water works, forest and a paper mill with a view to encouraging students to develop ideas for their project. Tutors sometimes take it upon themselves to take students to museums and the like. However, it is rare for ODL to be able to afford this luxury. Sometimes existing videos can be used to stimulate ideas and increasingly students may be able to resort to CD-ROM for inspiration.

Review

Students undertaking project work are typically anxious and overambitious. They are more likely to pick a project because of interest and give little thought to its feasibility. Students who are overambitious are more likely to have to change project topics part-way through.

Staff may facilitate the early stages of a project by providing a tutorial to allay students' fears, building in sufficient thinking time before students have to settle on a topic, stressing the importance of picking a feasible topic and insisting the topic is approved by a tutor before work begins. This may be formalized through an outline plan.

Points for reflection

What initial difficulties have the project students you have supervised had?
How far could you rely on written materials and scheduling devices to circumvent them?

Chapter 5

Collecting data

> The big problem is finding information.
> (ODL project student)

Locating information may involve delving in library reference sections; visiting archives, record offices, government departments, industry, schools, museums; undertaking field trips; interviewing and testing; writing to specialist societies; and combing databases.

A concern often expressed by staff, and one that deters many from offering more project work, is a fear that the outside world will not be cooperative enough to support students in their search for pertinent project data. Though success will depend partly on what type of data are being sought and how many students have trodden the same path, Open University experience suggests this fear may be exaggerated. Three-quarters of the open learning students I have studied managed to get what they felt was sufficient data for their project and most found the people they asked very helpful.

In project work the bulk of the student's time is normally spent collecting information for the project. (For example, in the OU study, on average students spent half their time collecting data for their project work.)

Sources of information

Students undertaking projects may seek help from many sources. In formal educational project s the student is likely to make use of libraries and interviews and be involved in various trips aimed at gaining information. Tough's (1967) research on 'individual learning projects' found that on informal projects his sample sought help, information or other assistance from an average of ten people, most of whom were fellow learners and friends rather than professional contacts.

Libraries

Most students undertaking a large project end up using a library if only to provide some background information on their project. Full-time students rely on the school or college library but part-time students make use of small branch, large reference and local university or college libraries. In the pre-database era, I estimate it was common for adult open learners to make as many as ten visits to a library in connection with their project in the late 1970s (Gains, 1977; Henry, 1978b). The increased availability of databases and keyword search systems has reduced the amount of leg work required for a literature search, but students often find they need to make a number of visits. Literature reviews are still an iterative process with one reference leading to another and so on.

Librarians are very well qualified, and often very willing to put their skills to good use helping a student locate relevant material (95 per cent of Open University students found staff in libraries and other public institutions helpful in this respect). The open learning student may be reassured by the OU study finding that about three-quarters of students found the large reference library sufficiently helpful. In contrast, less than a half found university, college or small branch libraries helpful. The same study suggested that the vast majority of students found more specialist sources like record offices, archives and parish registers helpful for their purposes. Alas the same cannot be said of approaches to national societies, where only a minority were satisfied with the response they received.

Interviews

It was very difficult to coax the respondent into conversation without giving pointers as to what I was after.
(ODL project student)

Yorkshire people may be outward in forging initial friendships but they don't like you poking around. The brewery chap positively shrunk in his seat when I asked what it cost.
(ODL project student)

Projects requiring students to interview members of the public report a slightly higher difficulty rate. My studies suggest around a third find this very or fairly difficult. Where the student is asked to do what seems like an unreasonable number of interviews the figure can rocket to something like two-thirds.

A substantial minority of students are worried by the prospect of interviewing, particularly, as is so often the case, where the interviews relate to social science or education projects and include personal information. Staff can help by teaching students the rudiments of interviewing, for example how to avoid leading questions, double questions and how to deal with reticent or over-talkative people.

Field trips

Students doing projects involving field trips often find they end up having to make more trips than they envisaged. The OU study found two-fifths of students undertaking undergraduate projects involving field trips had been on five or more field trips in connection with their project. For geology students this meant travel time alone used up an average of 25 hours and a quarter of the ecology students had spent over 40 hours travelling. In both cases this is more than the number of hours originally allotted for the project! Staff need to ensure they allow for travel time and students need to be warned to pick a site that is not too far away.

Difficulties

- Access
- Obtaining information.

Access

These sorts of agencies are snowed under enough without us bothering them.
(ODL social science project student)

If you can't find a local cache because the vicar won't allow you access, you have to go to the next parish or adapt and turn to local archives instead.
(ODL history project student)

I'd thought of a mentally handicapped and an able-bodied club for 8 to 14 year-olds and was going to interview parents but its not right, it'll raise their hopes.
(ODL community project student)

Some projects require access to institutions, for example to interview school children or people working in particular organizations. Staff often fear that it will be very difficult to obtain this kind of access. Where a student is going in cold this may indeed be so. But open learners often decide to work on projects in areas where they already have connections, for example the teacher decides to interview children in their school, the manager chooses colleagues in his or her organization, the student picks friends, the housewife contacts neighbours and the retired person talks to acquaintances from his or her local club.

Experience with projects requiring access to school children suggests this is less problematic than staff anticipate, though the OU studies have suggested 10 per cent to 25 per cent of students may still have difficulties. This is a much lower percentage than those reporting difficulties on other types of project.

Clearly if a number of students are likely to contact the same organization or school, access may best be coordinated through a staff member to ensure particular organizations and institutions are not approached repeatedly.

Nevertheless it is important to remember that access arrangements can take time. For example, even on a small project where students were asked to interview five businessmen, many students had to contact 15 or more firms before receiving an affirmative reply.

If a number of students are working on related projects in the same area they quickly get to learn which local companies or individuals are prepared to help.

Students also need to be willing to contact the appropriate people. A number of OU students undertaking a project about the needs of the handicapped were very reluctant to take up professionals' time to research a need they thought they were unlikely to be able to implement.

Obtaining information

> There just wasn't anything; I couldn't get plans or contact the individuals; it was impossible.
> (ODL architecture project student)

Locating appropriate material is rarely easy, particularly on large unstructured projects, where over half the students may be expected to find it very or fairly difficult to locate appropriate materials.

In the OU study, around half the students on projects based on information obtainable from libraries and other public sources of information found it difficult to locate information. Students relying on primary sources of information like archives, original records or field data reported the greatest difficulty, with around two-thirds having problems.

The main problem for the student relying on secondary sources is when the library or record office does not hold the information the student wants or when it does not exist. Other major difficulties are problems in determining exactly what is available, and delays in receiving information once its existence is determined.

Of the students who changed projects in my comparative study, a third cited difficulty in obtaining information as one of the main reasons, and a fifth cited lack of information.

One might expect rural students to be disadvantaged when it comes to locating information in that they might be further away from major public libraries, college and other specialist collections. However, I found no correlation between rural, urban and metropolitan residence and completion of project work, except on social and educational research projects where access to school children seemed more problematical in the larger metropolitan areas (Henry, 1978b).

Common pitfalls

- Workload underestimation
- Waiting time
- Side-tracking
- Opening hours
- Distance.

Workload underestimation

> It often takes longer to find and locate information than read and use it.
> (ODL project student)

> I've been all over London trying to find various things and going up so many dead-ends and the time gets shorter and shorter.
> (ODL project student)

> You don't know what you're going to come up against. If you've not done research before, you might find yourself down a blind alley and go further into it than you should, because you don't know whether you're down a blind alley or if it's a real lead you're following.
> (ODL project student)

Students new to project work and research are generally very naive about the amount of time it will take them to collect the data they need. Few realize they may spend as much time searching for the data as reading and assimilating them.

They are also often very naive about the availability of material and unprepared for the fact that the world is not necessarily willing to cooperate with their enthusiastic search. The typical student ends up making many more trips than expected. Some get downhearted at unexpected blind alleys.

Number of trips

> This project is more of a problem with the family; you're away in the evening doing research and on Saturday you're away in the library.
> (ODL project student)

One of the reasons students spend so much time obtaining information is the number of trips they make in order to find the relevant data. This ranged from around a minimum of ten to about 30 on the project courses I studied. Regardless of the absolute number, it is almost invariably many more than the student anticipated would be necessary. And unlike most open and distance learning materials, project materials invariably take students away from home.

The University of Surrey (1984) advises their education project students to remember that 'everything takes longer than you think' and that 'bad timing is the single most important cause of project delay and failure'.

Waiting time

> It took two months before they sent it.
> (ODL project student)

> I wrote first and they took three weeks to reply, then I wrote back asking for photocopies but that took another three weeks.
> (ODL project student)

> I had to write officially to get permission and then again when I was about to go. I was hanging around for five weeks.
> (ODL project student)

The tendency to underestimate the time needed to collect data is compounded by the failure to appreciate the amount of waiting time involved in dealing with the outside world. For instance, it can take weeks for a firm to reply to your letter, for an ordered part or article to arrive or to arrange access to a willing respondent, and months for a book to arrive from interlibrary loans.

The end result is that some 30 per cent of the students in my studies failed to get all the information they needed in time for inclusion in their project report and half wished they had starting collecting data earlier. As you might expect, there was a moderate (.2–.4) but significant correlation between the date students started collecting information and their attitude to the importance of starting earlier. Students are also more likely to have to change projects on courses where they have started too late to obtain sufficient information for their preferred project.

Start date

There is also a relationship between satisfaction with the amount of information obtained and the length of time over which it was obtained. (This refers to the time that passed between the start and finish of data collection, not the number of full-time equivalent days spent searching for it.)

On unstructured project courses, I found a relationship between the date on which students started collecting information, time spent collecting information, amount of information obtained and retrospective attitudes on the merits of starting earlier. Basically, students who started later were more likely to fail to get enough appropriate information and more likely to advocate starting earlier (Henry, 1978a).

Side-tracking

You start only knowing about the famous people. Then you discover 12 very interesting characters and you start tracking them down and end up with people well outside your period.
(ODL history project student)

Many students who undertake a large project get so absorbed that they put in many more hours than officially required. With large projects, I found around a fifth of students end up realizing they have collected far too much information, which has usually taken too much time and takes even longer to sift through (Henry, 1978b). Such diligence may seem laudable, but the danger is that the student puts so much effort into the project that there is not enough time left to give adequate attention to the rest of their studies. Half the students taking unstructured project components felt they had neglected their course work as a consequence (Henry, 1984).

Opening hours

The theme I have chosen is not well documented so I have not been able to get anything much from public libraries and I have to go to specialist libraries. As I'm working out of London and most of the information is in the centre, I have got to have time off work to come in and am very much limited in the time I can spend.
(ODL project student)

Part-time students face the additional problem that many institutions do not open during out-of-work hours or, when they do, they only open for a few hours a week. For example, public record offices may only be open from 10.00 am to

12.00 am and 2.00 pm to 4.00 pm. Even libraries may only open one evening a week, which may not provide sufficient time to get to grips with what is available. This can present a serious dilemma for the part-time student who is hoping to be able to complete their project in the evenings and at weekends. Many part-time students find the only way to get the data they want is to take holiday time. Adult students who cannot take time off work easily need to choose their sources with this factor in mind.

Distance

> I was doing my union, marvellous, I thought, near where I work and they'll give me the archives. Not at all. A couple of years ago they transferred most to Warwick and the rest to Colindale so I've got to spend my summer holidays in Warwick!
> (ODL project student)

Another factor worth bearing in mind is distance to the main source of information. This is particularly critical for the part-time student who cannot easily take time off work. So students in full-time work are well advised to check that there are relevant local sources available for their project.

Facilitative devices

Guidance on how to collect materials is traditionally offered by the supervisor on a one-to-one basis. The drawback with this approach is that it is an expensive resource. There is no doubt that students on the larger type of unstructured projects (which tend to range from around 50 hours upwards) find this kind of individualized help very useful. On the smaller project exercises, a lot of the advice needed to aid data collection is common to most students and can be documented and provided to successive students as written, audio or video material. This will include advice on interviewing and questionnaire design as well as information on relevant texts, databases and sources of information. Design factors that assist the data collection stage are:

- Materials
  - providing information on sources
  - offering a fallback project
- Scheduling
  - over a long period

- Assignments
  - requiring staged assignments
- Tuition
  - offering specialist tuition
  - arranging peer group support

Materials

Information sources

The project tutor can save time repeating information about sources of information by providing a bibliography and general information about where and how to find information. While some students are content to find their own way around the system, others welcome information of this type.

General information could include a guide on how to use libraries and what databases are available, a list of relevant national societies and local sources of information. Institutions may find it cheaper to provide the same or a very similar library guide for students on a number of different courses. Open University librarians have provided customized versions of the same basic guide for students, which highlight sources of information particularly relevant to the discipline concerned.

Other projects may require more specialized information. In a history project this might mean listing the whereabouts of public records offices and their opening times, and specialized national societies. In a social science project this might involve information on how to design a questionnaire and how to conduct interviews. Mace (1984) describes how staff on a distance-taught architecture and design project decided to increase the amount of advice they had originally included on finding information in libraries and public record offices in an attempt to speed up the time students were taking to get data.

Various project courses arm students with an official letter of introduction in an effort to help persuade librarians, archivists, officials and other personnel that students are engaged in a legitimate educational task.

Fallback project

Staff may also wish to consider whether or not it is appropriate to provide a fallback project using supplied data. This is a common device designed to cater for those students who, through no fault of their own, are unable to get sufficient data. Several Open University education projects offered interview data for those students unable to generate sufficient information themselves. Some studies suggest that the fallback option is not abused as take-up can be very low. For example, I found under 5 per cent of students needed to draw on this data, Bates

3 per cent (Crooks *et al.*, 1977), and Bynner (1975) found only 3 per cent using fallback data in an education project.

The Open University has also offered a number of courses where students were given the option of locating their own materials for their project or using some supplied by the course team. The latter option is likely to take less time. Perhaps surprisingly, only about a quarter of students on education and technology projects have opted to take the easy path and rely solely on materials supplied by the course team (Henry, 1978b, p.237, 244).

Scheduling

A simple design feature than can circumvent wasted waiting time is to schedule project work alongside other course work, rather than undertaking it in a block. This allows the student to get on with something else while waiting for the book, the next council meeting, clear day or whatever their project requires. Often projects are scheduled at the end of a course. The problem with undertaking the project at that point it that this rarely allows for the inevitable unexpected hitches that occur in projects, like waiting for particular data. Scheduling the project to start slightly earlier can help many students get round these problems. For example, one could suggest students begin to put in motion applications for key books and negotiating access no later than half-way though a year's course rather than leaving it to the last quarter. One way of doing this is to split the project work into several blocks slotted in at different points in the course; for example, a two-week block followed by a six-week block scheduled later in the course.

Assignments

A series of staged assignments can help focus the mind of a student with a tendency to become over-absorbed in his or her project or who is tempted to leave it until the end. Requiring students to submit an assignment on the sources used and discarded obliges them to start assimilating what they have and to begin organizing the material.

Tuition

Peer group support
A short meeting between students undertaking projects can provide a lot of moral support, as it quickly becomes apparent that everyone has a hard luck story about attempts to get information. A supervisor can also help reassure students that setbacks are a standard part of the research process. Students may also have picked

up a lot of local knowledge that can be helpful to their fellows; for example 'Don't bother to try company X, they don't want to know, but company Y was really helpful'.

Review

Collecting information takes up the bulk of the students' time – around half for students on unstructured courses. Students generally underestimate the amount of time needed, fail to appreciate the number of visits that will be necessary and are naive about the availability of relevant documents and the time needed to get them. Many put off data collection to a point where they leave themselves insufficient time to collect sufficient information.

Staff in libraries are often found to be very helpful; the chief difficulty with documented evidence is the absence of the desired information. With interviews, the main problem is difficulty in gaining access to appropriate people. Given a sensible approach, access to institutions is often less problematic than staff anticipate.

Staff can assist by providing a bibliography and indications of where to find information, and by encouraging the student to start the data collection period early and continue it over a long period.

Points for reflection

Think of a project you would like the learners in your charge to undertake.
What sort of information would they need for this project?
Is there any existing material you could provide to support their efforts?
Who could you ask to help provide specialist advice on data collection?

Chapter 6

Analysis and report writing

> Drawing it all together was a nightmare, but worth it.
> (ODL project student)

Data analysis in a project can take many forms. Often the student's task is one of organizing and interpreting the data. In an empirical research project the student is also expected to employ various other skills, such as the use of appropriate statistics. Most ODL projects are assessed on the basis of a submission which includes some form of written report.

The task of organizing, analysing and interpreting project data is considerably more demanding than organizing material for an essay or report. Teachers can expect about 60 per cent of their students to have difficulty with analysis, ie, more than the proportion reporting difficulty deciding on a topic or collecting data. In larger unstructured projects, like dissertations, this proportion may rise to as much as three-quarters.

Writing up a project seems to cause even more problems than any other stage, with over 60 per cent reporting difficulty. The proportion having problems tends to increase with the size of the project (Henry, 1978a, p.123). At this stage, students on many of the more structured projects report about as much difficulty as those on unstructured dissertation-like projects. Empirical projects are often perceived as even more demanding. It is not uncommon for four-fifths of open learning students undertaking projects requiring statistical or some other relatively sophisticated form of data analysis to report difficulty in writing up the material.

This problem is sometimes exacerbated by a lack of clarity about what exactly is required. Indeed I found significant correlations between the level of difficulty reported by students and the clarity about what was required of them in terms of writing up the report, in 16 out of the 20 courses I was studying (Henry, 1978b, p.97).

On an unstructured project, teachers can expect students to spend about a fifth of their study time attempting to organize, analyse and interpret their project data and a quarter writing up the project assignment.

On social science research projects which involve scoring, producing frequency counts and/or statistical analysis, I found this proportion rose to around a third of the total time spent for relatively simple analyses and nearer two-fifths of the time available for studies requiring more complicated statistical analyses (Henry, 1978a, p.81). Writing up also takes a little longer than on other kinds of projects (around a third of the total time on structured social research projects).

The total length of time taken to write a project report varies according to the length of report required. A 5,000–6,000-word report may be expected to take around 25 to 40 hours, a 3,000-word report 15 to 20 hours and a 1,500-word project 10–20 hours. However, students vary markedly in the length of time they take to write up project reports: I found 5,000-word reports took from 10 to 50 hours, 3,000-word reports anything from 5 to 30 hours and 1,500-word reports between 5 and 15 hours (Henry, 1978a).

Tutors should be aware that unless penalties are clearly spelt out at the start, a high proportion of students submit overlong project reports – anything up to twice that specified is not uncommon.

On structured projects it is often possible to anticipate or specify the kind of analysis expected and produce standardized guidance that will apply to most students, such as examples of how to set about analysing survey data, the elements of inferential statistics, etc. However, on unstructured projects it may not be possible to offer as much standardized advice, as the nature of the data obtained by the student and the context in which they were obtained may vary so much that individualized advice is also necessary. For example, I found only about a third of Open University students doing structured projects had bothered to obtain advice from their tutor, whereas two-thirds of those undertaking unstructured projects had needed advice from their tutor (Henry, 1978a, pp.82–3). This is not to imply that standardized written advice is unnecessary on unstructured projects; the same study showed four-fifths of students found the written advice offered on structured projects helpful compared to two-thirds of those undertaking unstructured projects.

The Open University, which offers variable amounts of tuition to students on project courses, found a surprisingly constant proportion of students – around two fifths on any given project course – who wanted more help from both their tutor and course materials to assist them organize, analyse and interpret their project data.

Similarly, students generally want help in determining how to write up their project. Some of this may be provided in standardized written form, but individual tuition is usually necessary in any substantial project. I found that three-quarters of students who were expected to produce 5–6,000-word reports wanted some individualized tuition, as did half the students submitting shorter unstructured project reports and less than half of those submitting reports on structured projects.

Difficulties

- Demanding nature
- Specialized knowledge.

Demanding nature

> Invariably the final report takes longer than anyone expects. (Tutor)

An unstructured project is a demanding task. While some students come into their own with this type of work, the weaker student can flounder and may need considerable help to complete the task. Some staff have got round this problem by offering two types of activity simultaneously, eg, a case study where all the materials are provided or a project where the student has much more freedom to choose the topic they want to work on and how to go about it. Often the weaker, less confident or busier student happily settles into the case study and the brighter, keener or more adventurous student is willing to invest the extra time the project will take for the freedom to work on something that interests them.

Specialized knowledge

> The course material did not equip us to cope with the sort of practical experience required for the project. Those of us without sufficient statistics are at a disadvantage.
> (ODL project student)

> The project required a much greater grasp of both formulae and computer usage than I had achieved.
> (ODL project student)

Some projects require specialized knowledge before the student can undertake analysis of the project. The classic example here is a social research project. Typically, skills of questionnaire design, interviewing, numeracy, basic computer literacy and statistical competence are simply assumed in projects of this type. Needless to say there are a number of different skills here which students may or may not have. (The point applies equally well to historical research students who may lack the requisite skills in historiography.) Lack of appropriate skills such as these is one of the reason students have difficulty completing projects. For example, in a survey of 43 journalism departments, Singletary and Crook (1986) found a third of respondents felt journalism Masters students had 'a great deal of difficulty completing theses'.

A sample of social research projects often reveals a disturbingly high proportion that are full of double-edged questions, presented by the interviewer in a leading manner and inappropriately analysed using, for example, a Pearson correlation when the data are nothing like an interval scale and certainly not normally distributed.

Students of this project type are usually particularly in need of help at the analysis stage. Staff need to provide assistance indicating appropriate statistics to use and allow time for students to familiarize themselves with this material. It takes quite some time to achieve functional usage of a simple computer statistics package, and time needs to be allowed for students to acquaint themselves with the requisite procedures, from familiarity with logging on and how to react to a given error message, to using the programme commands competently.

In short projects, analysis usually involves considerable demands on the tutor's time as students invariably need more help to analyse projects than with essays or reports.

Common pitfalls

- Misunderstanding
- Over-involvement
- Variability of source materials.

Misunderstanding

I found it difficult to assess exactly what standard was required for the analysis of the data and exactly what form the written analysis of the data should take.
(ODL project student)

Without a clear indication of what is required, a small proportion of students undertake analyses that are some way removed from what the teacher had intended. Sometimes this is not problematical but elsewhere such students may find their grading penalized.

Over-involvement

> To be able to make a good job of it you've got to spend time.
> (ODL project student)

Some students become entranced with the materials they discover and undertake a much more elaborate analysis and a much longer report than the task demands. Because they feel some ownership for their project and are studying an area of their choice, or simply because they get involved, many students studying projects end up devoting many more hours to the exercise than the teacher intended. This extra attention is laudable if time is unlimited but if it curtails other activities such as revising for exams, over-involvement can be a major problem. Some regular checks on progress can help here.

Alternatively, students may become so involved they want to do a wonderful report but for various reasons find it difficult to produce a report which reflects all the effort they have put in or which captures the wonders they have discovered as they would wish.

Variability of source materials

Project outcomes are not entirely predictable and regardless of the preparation and forward planning there are always some students who are fortunate enough to find lots of data or whose experiment works and others who are not so lucky and, despite all their best efforts, obtain null results or fail to obtain critical information. This will inevitably mean some projects are much easier to write up than others.

Facilitative devices

Tutors can help students by:

- Materials
  - offering written advice
  - providing sample reports
  - providing format guidelines
- Assessment
  - requiring a draft report
  - specifying assessment criteria
- Tuition
  - providing extra tuition
  - offering individual help.

Materials

Written advice
Teachers may need to offer quite a lot of advice to students undertaking empirical projects, especially those involving surveys or experiments. Some understanding of statistics is often necessary to do justice to this kind of project.

Sample reports

> An example project would help.
> (ODL project student)

Sample reports provide an excellent means of giving the students an idea of how to set about analysing the material they have collected. They also indicate the appropriate level of detail required. They are are invariably welcomed by students as they provide an excellent guide to the kind of thing required (Henry, 1978a; Hoare, 1980).

Format guidelines
Staff can assist students to write up projects in a number ways, most obviously by providing a suggested format which at least makes it clear to the students what sections are supposed to be covered in the report. This is particularly important in empirical research where a particular style of report is wanted.

In the OU study, three-fifths of students wanted format guidelines and a similar number wanted sample reports and discussion with their tutor. The latter figure was higher with unstructured than with structured project courses.

Assessment

Draft report
A draft report has two benefits. First, it acts as a pacing device, the existence of which encourages the student to start serious analysis and move towards some kind of closure. Second it provides an opportunity for feedback.

As discussed in Chapter 9, it is often a good idea to make the draft report non-assessed; that way students often feel freer to admit the doubts and uncertainties where they need advice. Students can feel pressure to submit a coherent logical plan if the draft report is assessed when what they really need is advice on how to deal with aspects of the data they are less sure of. Most students will take the opportunity to submit such reports.

Two-fifths of my OU sample felt assessment criteria would have been valuable and a quarter non-assessed draft reports. However, this rose to a half on courses where students had had the latter option. Less students favoured the idea of an assessed draft but again this figure increased to nearer two-fifths on courses that had offered experience of such a draft report.

Assessment criteria

Another important aspect is assessment criteria. It should be made clear to the students to what extent they are expected to relate the project report back to theory learnt elsewhere, how much of the detail of any empirical work is expected, etc.

There is one important criterion which is worth stressing in just about all projects. This is that the student is to be marked on the process not the product, ie, the way he or she set about tackling the project and not whether the outcome was positive or not. This criterion makes the process more equitable as the student who failed to obtain information or whose project went wrong in some other way then has the chance to obtain just as high marks as those whose project went well.

Tuition

Extra tuition and individual help

Students undertaking projects generally need more help from their tutor than they would undertaking other kinds of learning activities. This is just as true at the analysis and writing up stages as it is earlier in the enterprise. However, at this stage the tutor is often well advised to spend much of his or her time offering individual advice tailored to the needs of the particular student. Most students want help and, especially when it comes to writing up, benefit from some form of personal advice.

Review

Analysing the project data may be expected to take up around a fifth of the time spent, and writing up about a quarter of the total time spent (and often more on projects involving numerical analysis). Managing to organize, analyse and synthesize the information into a coherent and appropriate whole is a very demanding task, which often differentiates the weaker from the more able student. Most students need individualized help with sorting out their data on larger projects.

More students experience difficulty at the writing up stage of project work than any other and the time taken to complete this stage varies enormously between students. Staff tend to underestimate the time students take to write up projects and, for considered reports at college level, want to think in terms of something like 10 hours for a 1,500-word report, 20 hours for a 3,000-word report and 40 hours for a 5,000-word report. Fortunately the majority of students produce a better standard of work when submitting project reports than in other essays. This is largely because having some choice in the topic leads to a greater sense of ownership and preparedness to put in extra work.

Most students need assistance to get the best out of a project report. Giving report format guidelines and specifying assessment criteria helps, as does the provision of sample reports. Many students will also want individual help from a supervisor. The provision of a draft report in larger projects is also helpful. This is best non-assessed but for maximum take-up staff need to make a point of advising students to submit it. Since some projects will have been successful and others less so, it is very important that staff make clear they are grading the process, ie how the student tackled the project, not the product.

Points for reflection

What material will you provide to help your students analyse their projects?
Could any of this material be used for more than one course?
What format would you suggest students use to write up a project?
What criteria would you use to assess a project?

Chapter 7

Workload

You've got to put in time to make it worthwhile.
(ODL project student)

Many students are prepared to devote more time to a project than other learning activities and individuals also vary widely in the speed at which they complete projects, so the task of allocating an appropriate amount of time is not always easy.

Difficulties

- Overload
- Individual variation.

Overload

Time is more of a problem on a project-based course, it's not just a case of reading set books and recommended literature which are relatively easy to obtain, it is a question of deciding which project you're going to have, checking with the tutor to see if it's acceptable, then hunting for sources yourself to see if it's viable, then examining the source materials and reaching conclusions through an analysis and interpretation of the source materials.
(ODL project tutor)

One of the major problems with project work is the length of time it takes to complete. This applies to small structured projects as much as the larger unstructured project components. For example, three OU undergraduate social psychology mini-projects comprising an observation exercise, content analysis and an attitude scale were expected by staff to take about the same time as an ordinary essay, but actually took three to four times that long. An educational case study involving administering three tests or inventories to one individual and writing a report took three to four times as long as an essay, and a project requiring students to administer three questionnaires to a class and analyse the results took five to six times as long. Unstructured projects can expand indefinitely.

When I asked OU students to estimate an appropriate time allowance for their project, the average time suggested was generally slightly above the amount students claimed to have spent and much higher than the amount the staff had estimated (Henry, 1978a, p.120).

Another problem is the type of time: books can be read on the bus to and from work or college, and essays can be hurriedly completed late at night, but projects usually involve special trips at a time that suits the visitee, waiting time that is not easily compressed.

The overload caused by project work is often inescapable as projects are usually a compulsory part of a course and often account for a significant proportion of the final overall course grade.

Individual variation

> I'd much prefer to spend the time, because it is quite enjoyable and interesting, especially when you start to get somewhere.
> (ODL project student)

> I'd rather spend twice as long on a project, than plough through course units, especially if it is one of your own choosing.
> (ODL project student)

The individual variation in the time spent on project work is much greater than that found in other areas. For example, at the extreme, differences in the total time spent ranging from under ten hours to over 250 hours were found in over 12 project courses at the Open University (Henry, 1978b, p.152). This is only partly because some projects turn out to be much more straightforward than others.

Student enthusiasm is another part of the overload problem. Some students get so interested they spend the extra time out of sheer enthusiasm. Many reach a level of involvement where they do not begrudge the extra time as they are so absorbed in the process.

Such commitment sounds laudable, but part-time students who are working or have other commitments, and full-time students struggling with other aspects of their studies, can find the extra demands on their time very problematical.

Common pitfalls

- Time under-allocation
- Over-involvement.

Time under-allocation

A major problem is many teachers' inability to allow a realistic amount of time for a project. The time staff allocate for project work is all too often a chronic underestimation of the time needed to complete the task. Jankowicz (1991) provides estimates of the time required in Table 7.1.

Table 7.1 *Estimates of standard times for some project activities*

Reading an empirically-based journal article thoroughly	3 hours
Reading a book thoroughly	10 hours
Absorbing and using a statistically-based technique based on five texts	50 hours
	(with a total elapsed time of 8 weeks)
Preparing a ten-question interview schedule	1 day
Pre-testing the schedule on two interviewees and amending the result	1 day
Destroying a relationship through lack of pre-testing an inept interview schedule	1 minute
Conducting an interview	1 hour
Conducting four interviews in the same location (five possible, but very tiring)	1 day
Transcribing one hour of tape-recorded interview	7 hours
Cross-checking an interviewee's opinion or assertion	up to 4 phonecalls
Content analysis of 300 one-sentence written items already typed onto cards	7 hours
Reliability cross-checking of the result	6 hours
Final version: add another	2 hours
Informal pre-testing of a questionnaire by five respondents located on one site	1 day
Piloting a larger questionnaire more formally	up to 4 weeks
Pre-testing a single summated rating scale for internal consistency	2 days
Reaching postal questionnaire sample by first-class mail	1 week
Time for respondent completion	2 weeks

Time for postal return	1 week
Add lag time since many respondents peak at two weeks but some take longer	2 weeks
Time to post, complete, return chase-up letter and questionnaire	3 weeks
The 'psychological week' (at the **end** of which period, an enquiry to a respondent made at the **beginning** of the time will be forgotten)	5 days + weekend + 5 days
Creating a six-field (mixed numeric and textual) database ready for printout	4 hours
Filling the database with 50 records, each of 400 characters across six fields	5 hours
The sample size below which it probably pays to hand-analyse a simple 15-question questionnaire with no appreciable cross-tabulations	100 people
The sample size above which it usually pays to use a computer, even though you aren't familiar with the software in question	200 people
It all depends	100 to 200 people
Time taken to absorb SPSS manual sufficient to do one analysis, assuming you understand the basic statistical procedures involved but don't know SPSS	3 days

Source: Jankowicz (1991, Table 5.2, pp 66–7, Chapman and Hall).

Perhaps teachers forget just how long it used to take them to do projects when they first started this kind of work. Most students who are asked to do a large project have never done work of this kind on this scale before. Being unfamiliar with libraries and other sources of information, they are inefficient data-gatherers. Having little idea of the work they can reasonably expect to complete, many waste time by being overambitious. If they live some way away from their source of information, travelling time alone can take hours. In short, they will take much longer to complete a project than a teacher or academic who has been researching for years, has a good library two minutes from their office and is used to organizing diverse information into a long report.

Unfortunately the time staff allow is often driven by the limited time available in the curriculum rather than any realistic estimation of the actual work involved in undertaking the project. Estimates can be widely optimistic; for instance, an undergraduate geology project which involved deciding on a topic, collecting information (which invariably involved travelling to a site several times),

Course:	Geol	Pol	Arch	Hist	Stats	Inser	Pers	Com	Ed	Ecol	Syst	Psy	Env	Ed Pol	Mat
Ratio average time spent/ allotted	5	3	2	1.5	1.5	3.5	3.5	3	5	2	2	2.5	6	2	1 2
Hours allotted	20	36	80	160	50	21	20	20	10	36	30	20	6	24-31	70 10
Average number of hours spent	96	102	145	215	81	72	70	62	47	64	63	53	38	57	90 22

Source: Henry, 1978a.

Figure 7.1 *Overload on project courses*

analysing the data and writing a report, was allotted 20 hours. In fact, over a fifth of students spent 125 hours or more. Similarly, an education project that involved arranging access to school children, testing a class of 30 or administering three tests to one child, scoring the results, and analysing and writing a report, was estimated as needing 20 hours. Here, around a third spent over 50 hours (Henry, 1978b, pp.152, 275).

Open University experience suggests it is the smaller project that is least likely to be allotted a reasonable amount of time. For example, in three-quarters of projects allocated 21 hours or less, four-fifths of students spent over the time allowed. In those allocated over this amount, more than two-thirds spent extra time (Henry, 1978b, p.152).

I found a huge difference between the time allotted and that taken. Figure 7.1 summarizes the time allotted and average time spent on project work in some Open University project courses. In virtually every case the academics have chronically underestimated the time required and in two-thirds of cases they have underestimated the actual time spent by between two and six times! Three-quarters of the projects were overloaded by some 30 to 60 hours. (In all but six cases this is out of a 180-hour course). If it is objected that the average time taken may be inflated through the inclusion of extreme and atypical students prepared to work day and night on their projects, note that using the median rather than average produces a similar picture. For example, in a third of the projects the median time taken by over four-fifths of students was between three and a half and six times the number of hours allotted, (Henry, 1978a, p.117). This same study showed that between a third and two-thirds of students felt more time should have been allowed.

Despite widespread awareness of the findings of this study, many academics at the Open University continued to underestimate the time allowed for project work. For example, in the research methods course, the estimate was out by a factor of two (Bynner and Henry, 1984).

Over-involvement

There are quite large numbers of students who become so involved with their project work that they neglect the course work. Generally, the greater the overload the greater the percentage neglecting other aspects of their studies. Students in this position may neglect anything seen as peripheral, including readings, broadcasts, computer-assisted learning, etc.

This has an unfortunate knock-on effect. For example, half the students on seven courses and over a third on another seven in the OU study felt they had neglected their course work. I found a significant correlation between time spent and the percentage neglecting their course work on half the project courses in this study (Henry, 1978a, Figure 72; 1978b, pp.352–70).

The experienced project student expects to spend extra time conducting a project. For example, Hodgson and Murphy (1984) found that while most of their students had spent much more time on their project than they felt the project notes implied would be necessary, only 40 per cent said the work took longer than expected. It seems students can have a more realistic idea of the time needed to complete a project than staff!

Facilitative devices

Time allowed

- Realistic time allocation
- Apportion time appropriately

Schedule

- Starting early
- Running alongside course work.

Time

Realistic time allocation
The implications of these findings for those wanting a guideline for the amount of

time to allot a project might think in terms of at least 25 hours for structured projects and a minimum of 50 hours for the unstructured project.

Minimum study time
Structured project   25 hours
Unstructured project   50 hours

The reasoning behind this is the surprisingly constant average time spent on projects of a similar nature and size. For example, in Figure 7.1 we see that the average time spent on unstructured projects was never less than 60 hours, and on the larger project components never less than an average of 90 hours. Similarly, excluding the mini-project, no structured project involving collecting information took less than 30 hours. Allowing for the over-enthusiastic, a rule of thumb might be an absolute minimum of 50 hours for 3,000-word unstructured projects and 70 hours for 5,000-word ones; 25 hours for structured projects involving collecting information and 15 hours for case study projects that do not involve collecting information.

Appropriate time allocation

Although the average time spent on each phase varies, the proportion of total time spent on unstructured projects remains surprisingly constant.

Course developers may find it helpful to schedule the projects into the overall course timetable using the approximation that, on average, students spend 10 per cent of their time deciding what to do, 45 per cent collecting information, 20 per cent analysing and 25 per cent writing up.

Figure 7.2 shows the project study findings which support these guidelines. It is particularly striking that so many unstructured projects of such diversity in the amount of time allowed, scope and discipline should produce such constancy across stages.

Course:	A305	A401	D301	D331	D332	S323	S333	T262	TD342	P853	Range	Median
Deciding on topic	6	5	8	7	7	11	5	13	8	10	5–13	8
Collecting information	48	51	40	45	48	46	54	42	44	44	40–54	47
Analysing data	21	24	26	19	20	22	21	21	25	17	17–26	21
Writing report	26	20	27	28	25	21	20	24	22	29	20–29	25

Figure 7.2 *Percentage of time spent on each stage of unstructured projects*

There is more variation in the percentage of time spent at each stage on the structured projects. The main difference is that students spent less time collecting data, and on research projects which involved scoring or statistics, more time analysing the data, where the pattern is roughly 10 per cent deciding, 30 per cent collecting, 30 per cent analysing data and 30 per cent writing up; see Figure 7.3.

Course:	PE261	E201	E203	E341	D305	D291	Range	Median
Deciding on topic	7	9	7	13	7	3	3–13	7
Collecting information	43	25	34	15	34	32	15–43	33
Analysing data	23	34	23	40	29	33	23–40	31
Writing report	27	32	27	32	30	32	27–32	31

Source: Henry, 1987b.

Figure 7.3 *Percentage of time spent on each stage of structured projects*

Scheduling

Starting early

The temptation to fall behind with project work is particularly easy in open and distance learning. Working alone at home or trying to study part-time, in addition to a full-time job, means there are always many alternatives competing for the learner's time. A large percentage of open learning students get behind with their work. OU studies suggest 50 per cent may be expected to be behind at any given time. This is not critical for essay assignments where a learner can stay up late and catch up with a concentrated period of work. Because of the waiting time involved in projects, where students are waiting for other people to supply them with critical information, it is not always possible to complete projects in a concentrated burst. Further, because project work is often original, it normally requires more mulling-over time and periods where the student has to sleep on the material before they are ready to settle on a big project. So, the earlier it can be scheduled the better and the student really needs to ensure that he or she begins the work in good time.

Running alongside course work

The project has to be done in lumps – you can't take five names down at a

time, whereas generally you can study an hour here and an hour there.
(ODL project student)

Because of the mulling-over time time needed and more especially the amount of waiting time involved in gaining access and information for projects, there is a lot to be said for running a project component alongside course work rather than presenting it as an add-on at the end of the course. Students could carry out other course work during the waiting time involved in arranging access, obtaining materials and other tasks related to their project.

With a project-based course where all the assignments are projects, there may be a temptation to run different projects side-by-side. Open University experience suggests that this is not as successful as running projects alongside course work. A large project takes a certain amount of mental absorption that seems to complement course work but sits less happily with other large projects, at least for part-time learners. Students on the research methods course found it very confusing to have to do a qualitative project alongside a demanding quantitative project and the overwhelming majority favoured undertaking these sequentially (Henry, 1986).

Other pacing devices include the use of draft or staged assignments to encourage the student to start work, or requiring the student to contact the tutor and get him or her to agree on the suitability or otherwise of the chosen topic by a certain date (see Chapter 9).

Review

On most projects the amount of time allowed to do the work is a gross underestimate of that needed. Most students take much longer to complete the project than the number of hours specified. Substantial numbers get so involved with the project they neglect their other course work.

As a rule of thumb, 5,000-word unstructured projects should be allocated at least 70 hours; 3,000-word unstructured projects at least 50 hours; 3,000-word structured projects at least 25 hours and those that do not involve collecting information at least 15 hours.

Approximately 10 per cent of this time will be needed for deciding on a topic; 45 per cent for collecting information; 20 per cent for analysing data; and 25 per cent for writing the report. Research projects that involve scoring and statistical analysis need more like 10 per cent for deciding on topic, 30 per cent for collecting information, 30 per cent for analysis and 30 per cent for writing up.

Points for reflection

Imagine you are setting students a project.
How much study time would you allocate to this task?
What would you delete from the course content to provide this time?
When you do set a project, ask students to keep a record of the time they spend on it. Compare this with your estimate.

Section C: GUIDELINES

Chapter 8

Materials

Presenting projects to open and distance learning students needs careful planning as they are likely to have less face-to-face support from their tutor than the conventional student. In effect the teacher needs to anticipate many of the problems the student may have, exemplify what is required, advise the student on the possibilities, build in structures to support them and make certain the project is 'doable'.

Even staff who are philosophically disinclined to provide much structure (fearing this is a form of control that will inhibit students) have often found the need to introduce more structure over time. This trend seems to apply even in the extreme case of institutions committed to independent study and a project orientation. For example, the School for Independent Study at Lancaster found they had to be much more explicit about their criteria for assessment. The School for Independent Study at the University of East London introduced much more structure in the early planning stages, including training workshops (Percy and Ramsden, 1980). The University of Aalberg, which operates a project-based curriculum, has also now introduced more structured projects earlier in the curriculum (Olsen and Laursen, 1991).

Ironically, in terms of staff preparation time, the unstructured project is often less time-consuming than the structured one. Since unstructured projects are fairly open-ended they need less written support and are often supported only by a study guide outlining the procedure rather than providing content. Structured projects on the other hand often take a lot of preparation time, for example, collecting pertinent case study material, checking that a research design will work or that sources of data are available. Anecdotal evidence suggests that staff can take longer to prepare a structured project than conventional open learning material.

Not that unstructured projects are a soft option, as any saving in preparation time tends to be offset by the need to provide extra monitoring and facilitation of the students' projects. Kennedy (1982) points out that the learner-directed approach inherent in project work is neither unsystematic nor unstructured: 'It requires careful planning and monitoring by the tutor and a detailed framework of organisation'.

There are basically six ways to support open learning projects, through written material, audio-visual media, computers, assessment devices, tuition and scheduling. Scheduling was discussed in the last chapter; material, media and computing support are discussed in this chapter; and assessment and tuition in the ensuing chapters.

Students need to have a clear idea of what is entailed in the project at the outset. I found the Open University project courses rated as most difficult by students (which over a fifth found very difficult) were those where students were unclear what was expected. The difficulty derived from poor design, ie, a vague description or a confusing one, a demand for statistical competence among the non-numerate, or a creative response in areas that were utterly new to students (Henry, 1978b, p.166).

Written material

In an open learning project the teacher needs to pre-specify a lot of the things a tutor might normally be able to discuss with the student in person. This entails:

- offering extra guidance
- forewarning students of pitfalls
- providing a fall-back project.

Offering extra guidance

Students undertaking project work are often given very little in the way of back-up support material. This is a pity as studies suggest that where such support is offered it is much appreciated, provided it is relevant to undertaking the project. As shown in Figure 8.1, the OU study found two-thirds of students wanted more written help to write up their project (presumably on the expected format). Just under half wanted written help with analysing material; this proportion rose slightly to just over half on the survey projects requiring numerical analysis, whereas only around two-fifths wanted the extra written assistance to help choose their project topic and collect data.

	Unstructured	Structured
Deciding on topic	38	37
Collecting information	40	37
Analysing data	42	48
Writing up	65	67

Figure 8.1 *Percentage of students wanting more help with project from course material*

Section B has already given some indication of the type of information and guidance required; this is summarized below:

Type of guidance required

To indicate scope: list project topics and provide sample projects

To assist data collection: list type of material and institutions, offer guide to local and national sources

To assist data analysis: demonstrate techniques and methods

To assist project report: provide format guidelines, assessment criteria and sample reports.

Topic list
First the student needs help with deciding on a topic. In addition to a general description of what is required, some project courses offer an indicative list of possible topics. The fear that adult open learners will merely copy one of these topics seems ill-founded. Such students have had time to develop interests and very rarely opt for one of the suggested topics, but they find a list of sample topics valuable as an indicator of the type of topic expected (Henry, 1978b).

Some project courses go to greater lengths. The OU design course 'Man-made Futures' provided its students with a game designed to help them decide on a topic; it has to be said this met with mixed reaction.

Data source information
Distance learning students need some indication of where they can be expected to find appropriate material. For many humanities projects this will largely comprise local libraries, public record offices and any national societies pertinent to the

Figure 8.2: Extract from Information Search Guide

Abstracts and indexes

Review articles
.....

Research in Organizational Behaviour,
Research in Personnel and Human Resources
Management,
Studies in Management Science and Systems,
Studies in the Management Sciences.
Or reviews may appear in the normal academic
journals, i.e.:
Done, D. (1987) Essay review: information
technology, *Long Range Planning*, vol. 20, no. 1, p.
134-143.
Meidan. A. (1986) Handbook of business policy,
Management Decision, volume 24, no. 4, p. 1-123.
Rothwell, S. (1986) Planning for human resources;
essay review article, *Long Range Planning*, vol. 19,
no. 5, p. 109-112.
Many of the abstracting services list reviews
separately. *Current Contents in Social and
Behavioral Scienccs* (see below) prints the
contents pages of the latest volumes of the main
review series.

Conference papers

Conferences, by bringing together people who
may be from different disciplines and occupations
to report academic progress or new approaches to
a problem, are often a good place to hear of fresh
thinking in a field. Unfortunately the published
proceedings can take years to appear.
Some abstracts and indexes list conferences
separately and index the papers like journal
articles. There are also specialised services
through which you can find out if the proceedings
of a particular conference have been published,
whether there have been recent conferences on
particular topics, or whether papers on your
subject have been given. Most libraries will take
one of these and the proceedings listed in the
British Library's *Index of Conference Proceedings
Received* are all available through the inter-library
loan service.
In cases where the proceedings have not been
published, you can of course try approaching an
author or sponsoring organisation directly.

Theses

If you wish to trace a particular thesis or find out if
one has been written on a subject, then there are
various indexes:
* *British Reports, Translations and Theses Received
by Thc British Library Lending Division* (all theses
indexed are available via the inter-library loan
system).
Dissertations International, monthly, University
Microfilms International (Doctoral and Post-
Doctoral; copies of the theses are available from
UMI).
*Index to Theses Accepted for Higher Degrees by the
Universities of Great Britain and Ireland and the
Council for National Academic Awards*, two a year,
Aslib.

In some cases, the permission of the author or of a
university body may be needed before a thesis
can be seen.
University Microfilms International (30 Mortimer
Street, London WlN 7RA) issues free catalogues,
on, for example, *Business and Management.
Management Science, Marketing, Operations
Research.*

Citation Indexes

The *Social Sciences Citation Index*, instead of
using subject headings. bases its indexes on the
references which appear at the end of journal
articles. It tells you who has referred to a particular
paper. Look up a key paper or book in the Citation
Index section: if you were interested in the
analysis of organisation structures, you might
choose Pugh. D. S. *et al.* (1968) Dimensions of
organization structure, *Administrative Science*
Quarterly, volume 13, p. 65-105. The Citation Index
will give you a list of articles which have included
the Pugh paper in their bibliographies and which
therefore presumably discuss the subject. The
Source Index contains full details of the citing
papers and their bibliographies, e.g. Gustafson, H.
W. and Hayden, S. J. (1985) Expert consensus in
prioritizing and scaling organization design
factors, *Human Relations*, *vol.* 38, no. 7, p. 665-681,
33 references (which are given in full).
This novel approach can turn up relevant articles
from unexpected disciplines. It also provides a
way of searching *forward* in time, of following up
discussion and argument.

'Current Contents'

If you want to keep track of what is appearing in
the latest issues of journals or review publications
which you have not got at hand, then 'current
contents' type publications will help. By
reproducing contents pages, they fill the time gap
between publication of a journal and the indexing
of its articles in the abstracts and indexes. They
usually have keyword subject indexes. If you come
across a likely sounding article, you can obtain it
as a photocopy via the inter-library loan service:
Contents Pages in Management, fortnightly,
Manchester Business School Library.
Current Contents: Social and Behavioral Sciences,
Institute for Scientific Information, weekly
(sections on "Economics and business" and
"Management").
Management Contents, fortnightly, Find/SVP
(contents pages of 375 journals; some American
bias).

4.5 Computer databases

The abstracts and indexes marked with an
asterisk, and, increasingly, the complete text of
newspaper and journal articles, are available for
online searching via a computer terminal.
Online searching makes a wide range of sources
aecessible; it is fast and it offers the capacity to
specify a subject in great detail; but it costs
money.

Various 'hosts' (e.g. DIALOG Information Services in America, the British Library's BLAISE service, Profile Information and Pergamon InfoLine in England, the European Space Agency's Information Retrieval Service in Rome) offer a range of 'files' for searching. It is with these hosts that arrangements over payment, passwords, etc. are made. Costs depend on the amount of time you spend connected to the computer and on the number of references, abstracts or articles you have printed out on- or off-line. Usually there is no subscription - you only pay for actual use. A search will typically cost between £8 and £30, but could be cheaper, or, particularly on some of the business databases, considerably more. Many of the UK organisations which use these online information retrieval services will do searches for the public. They may pass the charges directly on to the outside user or make a fixed charge. The Science Reference and Information Service offers a computer search facility at cost plus £15.

An advantage here is that many of the references retrieved will actually be found on the shelves. Some public libraries offer a subsidised service. The B.I.M.'s Management Information Centre charges £20, plus online costs.
If you cannot do online searches within your own organisation and you have your own microcomputer, modem and suitable software, you might like to investigate the service being developed by DIALOG for the individual user (details from knowledge Index.x, PO Box 8, Abingdon, Oxfordshire OX13 6EG). Providers of business databases are all keen to encourage their direct use by managers.
Few of the bibliographic files go back further than the 1970s. Printed sources have to be used for older material, though naturally recent writing refers you back to earlier work.........

Source: Open University Information Search Guide

Databases
Electronics

INPCC 3 000 000 records.
Institution of Electrical Engineers. The most important database for physics, electrical engineering, electronics, telecommunications, computers and control, and IT.
Covers journal articles, conference papers, reports, patents, books, theses.
Thesaurus: Inspec Thesaurus 1987
Printed equivaknt: Physics Abstracts; Electrical and Electronic Abstracts; Computer and Control Abstracts; IT Focus.

Materials

Metadex 700,000 records.
ASM International and The Metals Society. The most important database for metals and metallurgy: materials, processes, properties, products, forms, influencing factors, alloys, intermetallic compounds & metallurgic systems. Covers journal articles, conference papers, reports and books. *Pnnted equivalent: Metals Abstracts, Alloys Index.*

World Aluminium Abstracts
ASM International. 126 000 records.
Aluminium industry, ores, alumina production and extraction, melting, casting, metal-working, fabrication, finishing, metallurgy, properties and tests, quality control, end uses.
Journal articles, patents, government reports, conference papers, theses, books.
Printed equivalent: World Aluminium Abstracts.

Rapra Abstracts 250 000 records.
Rubber and Plastics Research Association of GB Processing technology, polymer synthesis, properties and testing, compounding, chemical modification, machinery, intermediate and semi-finished products, applications of polymers, hazards and toxicology, environmental effects, markets and industry.
Journal articles, trade literature, standards, reports, books, conference papers.
Thesaurus: Thesaurus of Controlled Descriptors.
Other databases cover paper and papermaking, and textiles.

Source: Adapted from OU Technology Project Information Guide

Extract from Information Search Form

SEARCH PROFILE FORM
(please fill in and send to us)

What subject do you wish to investigate

Key words you have selected

• Arrange in concept groups.

• Indicate which are 'official descriptors' and give the source where you found them.

Do you want only English references?

Source: Adapted from Open University Technology Project Information Search Form

Extracts from Regional Library Listing

University Libraries

(23)
QUEEN, MARY COLLEGE
(UNIVERSITY OF LONDON)
327 Mile End Road   Tel: 071 975 5555
London E1 4NS

Scope: General and 19th and 20th century diplomatic history.

Access: At librarian's discretion. For occasional use students can have admission to library and sign visitors' book. For longer periods of use, apply for permission, using OU letter of introduction.

Hours: Term: 09.00-21.00 Mon-Fri; 10.00-16.00 Sat
                        Vacation: 09.00-17.00 Mon-Fri.

(24)
SCHOOL OF ORIENTAL AND AFRICAN STUDIES
(UNIVERSITY OF LONDON)
Thornhaugh Street   Tel: 071 637 2388
Russell Square   See list below for extensions
London WC1H 0X9

Scope: The humanities and social sciences with regard to Asia and Africa in all languages.

Access: If available for studies relating to Asia or Africa, an application form for reference use should be obtained from the library. It requires the official stamp of the Open University and signatures of two staff.
                        Initial applications should be made during weekday office hours, where possible (Mon-Fri 0900-1700). Advice may be obtained from the following specialist librarians:

Africa: M.D. McKee (phone ext. 304)
Maps: Mrs. H. Holyoak (ext. 277)
Middle East (Islamic): G. Schofield (ext. 299)
Middle East (non-Islamic): P. Salinger (ext. 298)
South East Asia: Miss H. Cordell (ext. 313)
South Asia: R.C. Dogra (ext. 300)
Japan and Korea: B. Hickman (ext. 310)
China and Tibet: J. Lust (ext. 311)
Social Sciences, Law and General: A. Sabin (ext. 270)
Periodicals: Miss R. Stevens (ext. 302)

Hours :   Term: 09.00-20.45 Thursday, 09.00-19.00 Friday, 09.30-17.00 Saturday

(Closing 17.00 during Christmas and summer vacations)

Specialist Libraries

(30)
BRITISH ARCHITECTURAL LIBRARY
THE ROYAL INSTITUTE OF BRITISH ARCHITECTS
66 Portland Place   Tel: 071 580 5533
London W1N 4AD

Scope: Probably the most comprehensive collection on architecture in existence. Reference library of 92,000 vols.; unique collection of at least 250,000 drawings, membership records and archives, and manuscript holdings.

This library is much used and OU students would be well advised to have thought out their research area before making an approach so as to derive maximum value from specific queries.

Access: By letter of introduction from the Region.

Hours: 01.30-17.00 Mon, 10.00-20.00 Tues, 10.00-17.00 Wed-Fri, 10.00-13.30 Sat

(31)   BRITISH MUSEUM NATURAL HISTORY LIBRARY
         Cromwell Road   Tel: 071 589 6323
         London SW7   Gen. library Ext. 382
                                      Botony lib. Ext. 491
                                      Entomology lib. Ext. 530
                                      Palaeontology lib. Ext. 207
                                      Zoology lib. Ext. 272

Scope: Comprehensive book and periodical collections in all fields of geology. Map
          collection of 40,000 items. Comprehensive range of books and periodicals in
          ecology, located in general library, botany library, zoology library.

Access: For reference purposes when Readers Ticket has been obtained (application form
          available from the library). Personal reference from a Tutor or other recognised
          person necessary.

Hours: General library: 10.00-17.00   Mon-Sat
          Dept. libraries: 10.00-16.30   Mon-Fri.

Source: Adapted from OU London Regional Library Guide

Extract from Specialised Resources Guide

Record Offices

3.   THE PUBLIC RECORD OFFICE
          Kew Section   Ruskin Avenue,Kew, Richmond,
                                        Surrey TW9 4DU
                                        Tel: 081 876 3444

          Open: Mon-Fri 09.30-17.00 (but no requisitions for documents after 15.30)

          Records of present and defunct Government departments including Cabinet,
          Treasury, Admiralty, Foreign Office, War Office etc.

          Chancery Lane section   Chancery Lane,London WC2A 1LR
                                        Tel: 081 876 3444
                                        Hours as at Kew.

          Contains the early records, 11th Century onwards, especially judicial and
          administrative archives, the records of the State Paper Office, and, most usefully
          for D301 students the Census returns (enumeration books) for 1841, 19851, 1861 and
          1871. Readers are normally expected to use microfilm copies of these.

          The PRO closes for stocktaking for two weeks every autumn.

4.   THE OFFICE OF POPULATION, CENSUSES AND SURVEYS
                                        St. Katherine House, 10 Kingsway
                                        London WC2B 6JP
                                        Tel: 071 242 0262

          Open: Mon-Fri 08.30-16.30 Please make an appointment.

          Registrations of births, marriages and deaths in England and Wales since 1837.
          Full collection of printed census material for Britain and other countries.

5.   THE BRITISH LIBRARY
                                        Humsnities and Social Sciences
                                        Great Russell Street, London WC1B 3DG
                                        Tel: 071 636 1544
                                        (Reading Room admissions)

          Open: Mon, Fri, Sat, 09.00-17.00 Tues, Wed, Thurs 09.00-21.00

          Access only as last resort with very specific ticket applications. Ask your tutor or
          London regional Office for a reference.

          Official Publications Library
          This department houses official publications including Parliamentary Papers, and
          printed census reports.

Source:s Adapted from OU London Region Brief Guide to Archive and Research Resources in London particular area. Open learners appreciate names, addresses and telephone numbers so they can plan their visits in advance.

Students may also appreciate some indication of how to find their way around a library, the databases they can access, an introduction to the indexing system and an overview of key abstracts and reference texts and journals in the field. Librarians are often very willing to provide this kind of service. A booklet describing information sources can be given to students on many different courses or fairly easily customized for each, so in the long run it can save staff time. Illustrations of the type of information the OU has provided are given in Figure 8.2. Commercial abstracting and indexing services plus databases on CD-ROM are also available (eg, Bowker Sauer catalogue).

Over a period of years students and tutors may build up knowledge about organizations in the area which are willing to assist students with their project and those that are not. In conventional institutions this information passes along the grapevine like wildfire, but in open and distance learning there may be less opportunity for this transfer of information. A 'Sources of information guide' could usefully include students' comments and advice on how best to approach certain institutions and which ones to avoid.

Data analysis and report

At the analysis stage students need some indication of what to do with their data. There is great scope for demonstrating appropriate methods of analysis through ODL materials. Research projects may need quite a lot of support at this stage. Staff may be able to recommend a book which covers the necessary ground. For example, Bell (1993) describes some of the typical research procedures used in projects in a book originally developed in the context of open learning, and many psychology departments use Greene and D'Oliveira's (1982) excellent statistics book as a teaching text. In other situations staff may need to prepare material especially. For example, the OU research methods course included a detailed evaluation of two pieces of research on crime, designed to demonstrate the type of approach required for an evaluation project.

All students also need some guidelines on the expected report format and assessment criteria. They also appreciate the opportunity to peruse other students' sample reports. Some course teams abbreviate two or three of these and send them to students. Others hold a stock of such reports for loan or make them available at a particular time, eg, at residential school.

Forewarning students of pitfalls

Students working in isolation benefit from quite explicit warnings about the common pitfalls in project work. Some of the key points that apply to most projects are:

- check the information is available
- do not be overambitious
- pick a site near home/work
- start collecting information early
- avoid being side-tracked
- avoid neglecting other course work
- forewarn of possible expense
- encourage students to contact their tutor
- encourage students to submit non-assessed outlines and draft reports.

The reasons for these warnings are elaborated elsewhere in this book. For example, as explained in Chapter 4, students need to be encouraged to check that information will be available and pick a feasible project topic. They need to be encouraged to narrow down their choice to one smallish area that can be covered in the time available. The importance of picking a local site, starting collecting information early and the dangers of side-tracking and neglecting other course work are elaborated in Chapter 5. The importance of contacting the tutor and ways of encouraging this are elaborated in Chapter 10.

Expense

Projects can involve students in expenses they do not normally incur, for example, the travel costs associated with field visits and interviews, the telephone costs of arranging access and finding out what is available, the cost of copies of documents, postage, equipment, materials, books, journals, presentation folders and photographs. It seems only fair to warn the student of possible expense. About a third to a half of the students on three-quarters of the projects in the OU study felt they should have been warned.

Personal projects

> If I had known I had to tell my tutor all my thoughts I wouldn't have taken it.
> (ODL project student)

> I object to self-analysis; these are very personal thoughts.
> (ODL project student)

Many management and social science projects deal with very sensitive material and require students to undertake an analysis of themselves. Most students are more than happy to discuss their strengths and weaknesses in a project assignment but a significant minority find this very difficult, if not an unreasonable demand. With such projects it is important to make clear their personal nature at the outset. Tutors must also be very careful that they mark such projects sensitively, concentrating primarily on the way the project has been written up. Here it is a good idea to stress the importance of confidentiality. Students can be encouraged to use pseudonyms where necessary and tutors should respect the confidentiality of the material, avoiding showing the project report to other students, for example.

Providing a fall-back project

There are a number of situations where students might need fall-back projects, notably where students may end up with inadequate data through no fault of their own, and some course designers offer such fall-back projects. In research projects this will normally require students to analyse simulated data or a collection of case study materials. In humanities and other projects where these are not easily provided, the fall-back project may be of a different nature, for example a literature review. The OU geology course allows students having great difficulty finding information to use summer school data instead.

The housebound or prisoners are two more groups that may be unable to complete the original project and need a fall-back. Teachers have provided satisfactory projects for people in such positions by designing a project around items on television, newspapers or magazines. Staff sometimes fear students will be tempted to opt for the easier fall-back project; in fact various studies at the Open University suggest students rarely take this option. However, students are not always so obliging. The OU evolution course provides a compromise, offering students the choice between four two-stage projects. The first stage involves an experiment, field work or a computer simulation analysis. For the second stage of the field-based projects, students are given the option of further practical work or an essay and the majority choose the easier option of the essay (Hodgson and Murphy, 1984).

Audio-visual media

Audio-visual material can be used to support projects in a number of ways, notably as a tutorial about what is involved, to offer training in specific techniques and through illustrative case studies. I found students had a marked preference for programmes that followed other students' experience rather than teachers telling the student what to do, whether these involved case studies or group discussion.

Where access to video and computer-based equipment is limited, it would obviously be inappropriate to use these media to carry a major part of the teaching. Audio-visual media can be used to support projects via:

- explanation
- case studies
- training/demonstration
- tutorials.

Explanation

Programmes dealing directly with how to set about the project may be little more than talking heads, or they may involve interviews with learners who have undertaken similar exercises in the past. They have covered a discussion of what is expected, advice on how to choose a project, suitable data sources and feedback on past results.

An area that is rarely dealt with but one which I found students wanted addressed was a programme on how to write up the project. Recollections of past students' experiences of getting over the pitfalls can be very reassuring.

It seems students are much more likely to be interested in programmes reporting back aggregate data from their group if these are fed back to them while they are still involved in doing the project rather than afterwards (Crooks *et al.*, 1977). If timing precludes this possibility, students may appreciate a summary of the past year's aggregate data instead.

Training

Programmes on methodology often deal with various research procedures such as statistics or modelling, aspects of experimental and questionnaire design, ways of undertaking content analysis and structuring case study material. These can have an advantage in that they may be used for other purposes. For example, many projects involve interviews and could share a programme outlining appropriate ways of interviewing. One I produced myself involved extracts from particularly difficult interviews and used a freeze-frame technique to involve students in determining how they would respond at particular points. The programme went on to outline appropriate strategies.

The OU research methods course used several audio-visual programmes for this purpose, for example a broadcast TV programme of an ethnographic interview which students were asked to analyse for a formative assignment prior to conducting their own ethnographic project. Students also received a transcript of the interview and a second programme showed the course team's analysis. A radio programme offered further reflections on the ethnographic analysis provided and another gave background on a further project topic.

Tutorial

It is is also possible to broadcast live phone-in tutorials in which a group of students ask tutors advice about their project, for example. The OU research methods course used a radio broadcast to take phone calls from students and offer advice on the topic of hypothesis formulation and statistical analysis in connection with their project. With small groups, teleconferencing can achieve the same end.

Computers

Computers can be used to assist project work in a number of different ways, including:

- word-processing
- databases
- tutorials
- data-processing
- conferencing.

I could not get the computer terminal to do what I wanted it to do; at one point I took an hour to log on! I'm right off using a computer ever again. (ODL project student)

It is important to bear in mind the user-friendliness of the system where learners are not computer specialists. A non-user-friendly system invariably throws up problems students do not know how to deal with. Time should be allowed for students to acquaint themselves with the system. Ideally the student needs a telephone number and someone to ring when they get stuck.

Word-processing

Educators and trainers often expect projects to be typed and presented beautifully. Word-processing packages obviously ease this task and allow the student to store data, reorder, amend and style as desired. Some students also use a graphics package to help illustrate their project work. Most computers that offer word-processing and graphics also offer a spreadsheet facility. Students undertaking large projects or having difficulty pacing their work may find using a spreadsheet to plan and monitor progress helpful.

Databases

Many learners with access to a relevant computerized database find it easier to start their search for material relevant to their project there. Most systems have a keyword search facility. In library databases this may just search the title and author or, in the more advanced systems, will search the complete text. Students undertaking a large project may find it well worth searching some of the national and international databases such as DIALOGUE even if they have to pay a fee for this service. Increasingly, students can search databases like ERIC for free on their library's copy of the CD-ROM version. Most project students will be able to access whatever systems their library already provides.

Tutorials

Computers can also be used to assist project based learning by providing tutorials on particular topics. For example, the OU has used SAMP, a package designed to teach students about sampling, and CICERO, a computer-assisted learning package to provide back-up tuition in statistics.

Specialized topics such as statistics are particularly suitable for computer-assisted learning. Ideally the system is intelligent and when the student makes an error it provides further questions to assist him or her in grasping the point, or enables the student who has grasped the material to proceed at a faster pace. However, this kind of sophisticated program that operates at several levels is more expensive to design and implement. If the computer-based tutorial consists of little more than multiple choice questions with yes or no answers, pencil and paper presentation is probably a much cheaper way of achieving the same end.

Data-processing

Complicated data often benefit from the more sophisticated forms of analysis that are readily provided by a computer, the obvious example being to use a statistics package such as SPSS, SAS or PSTAT to analyse data. For students with only rudimentary statistics knowledge some staff prefer to offer a simple tailor-made user-friendly package offering a few key descriptive and inferential statistics. For more advanced students with some knowledge of statistics, it is often easier to arrange for students to access whatever statistics packages the institution or organization already has on-line. However, beware; staff nearly always need to provide back-up material explaining how to log on and access the material and some interface document which translates the statistics and computer manuals into a language comprehensible to learners. If a standard package is used then students can use knowledge gained on one project in analysing their next project.

The non-computer-literate may find it easier to use a statistical calculator than take the time that is needed to acquaint themselves with the relevant computer package.

Conferencing

Computer conferencing is one way in which geographically dispersed learners can keep in contact. Students sometimes use such systems to discuss assignments, including projects, for example, to see if someone else is undertaking a project in a related area or to discuss which companies or local schools are happy to help and which not and so on. Dirckinck-Holmfeld (1991) discusses an attempt to support distance students at the University of Aalborg where 50 per cent of teaching is undertaken through project work. As is so often the case with computer conferencing, only a subset of students were active members of the conferences.

Piloting

In a conventional institution there is usually ample scope for an on-going dialogue between the tutor and student in which any looseness in the original project proposal or design can be modified and tightened up over time. Such luxury is rarely possible in open and distance learning, so course designers need to be doubly certain they have anticipated the possible pitfalls and are offering a project that students will be able to do. The best way to ensure this is to pre-test the material through some kind of pilot. Students willing to pilot test material are often offered a reduced fee in return.

Advantages of piloting a project are that it:

- checks the time required
- ensures feasibility
- checks that local sources are available
- provides feedback on support material
- indicates extra guidance necessary.

The pilot need only be carried out with a few students; however, to be effective the students should attempt to do the project, not merely comment on the materials. Experience with various project courses suggests that if tutors or students merely comment on the material they will tend to accept the project authors' estimate of time and ready availability of source material. If students actually try to use the materials to carry out the project assignment, unanticipated problems are invariably identified. The four most common ones are:

1 The material is not as easily available as staff anticipated.
2 The project takes the students much longer to complete than staff anticipated.
3 Students are not completely clear what is required.
4 The students want more help.

The degree to which staff estimates of the time needed differs from that actually taken is often a shock to staff. More important, such information can help staff begin to think more realistically about the practicalities of trying to locate source material. For example, a statistics course had presented open learning students with a series of assignments based on various sources of publicly available data. They believed these data would be fairly readily available in the larger public and college libraries. In fact, piloting showed that this was not necessarily the case, and that some of the references were much harder to locate than others. It was relatively easy for these course designers to change the assignments to draw on the more readily available texts and suggest alternatives – a process that saved the students hours of worry and misplaced agony merely trying to locate the relevant source material.

In a research project, more preparatory work may be required. For example, a research course wanted its students to have first-hand experience of survey research and analysis. Students were presented with a structured questionnaire and were asked to collect four interviews according to a specified quota. These responses were then combined with their fellows to provide a larger data pool. These data were made available to the students. They were free to select their own hypotheses and asked to justify the selection of variables and statistical tests they used.

Combining the data with their fellows and the responsibility of choosing their own hypotheses, variables and mode of statistical testing made the exercise seem completely real from the students' point of view. In fact the course team had spent a long time developing and piloting a questionnaire to be sure it would work for students. For example, the team retained certain items and deleted others to ensure that they did discriminate between different types of respondents. This may seem like a lot of work to undertake for a student project, but since this project has been running for a number of years, it has also provided valuable data in its own right.

Piloting this project also showed the course team that they needed to provide more focused advice on inferential statistics to support the project.

Review

In designing projects for open and distance learning, teachers can expect to pre-specify more than they would in conventional learning situations. Research suggests staff are not very good at estimating the pitfalls students will face, so it is strongly recommended that all projects are piloted by a few students who actually carry out the project, where at all possible. Guidance on possible topics and information on where to find appropriate information, how to collect and analyse data, are appreciated by students. Much of this information, for example on library use, interviewing and statistical analysis, can be used for students on different project courses. Sample reports help students realize the appropriate scope and draft assignments help pacing. In some areas it is necessary to provide a fall-back project, for example of simulated data, for students who are unable to find sufficient data.

Audio-visual programmes can be used to support project work. Students often favour an approach that caters for students talking about their experience rather than staff telling them what to do.

Access to a computer can aid report presentation considerably. Databases make literature searches much simpler. Computers can also be used in the analysis of project data. With large numbers of students (ie, hundreds), computer-assisted learning may be useful to train students in project-related skills such as statistical analysis.

Points for reflection

What written material will you need to prepare to support your open learning projects?
How long do you think this will take you?
Could you use audio or video to support your project students?
What computer facilities can you use to support your project students?
Which students can you get to pilot this material?
Can you offer them reduced fees?

Chapter 9

Assessment

It's a much better test of ability and certainly sorts out the sheep from the
goats.
(ODL project tutor)

Projects are often a compulsory part of the curriculum and can account for a
significant proportion of the overall course grade. For example, in a survey of 60
engineering departments, Allison and Benson (1983) found the final year project
typically accounted for between 10 and 25 per cent of the overall course grade but
in some cases as much as 45 per cent.

Assessment method

There are two common approaches to assessing project work: use of a *final report*
and *staged* assessment. Either the project is assessed on the final report or, in the
staged approach, different aspects of the project are assessed in different
assignments. A much improved refinement on the final report system is to
ensure the student gets a chance to submit an outline and draft report before
submitting the final report. Independent marking gets a tutor other than the
student's supervisor to mark the final report. The use of a final report, draft and
staged assignments is illustrated overleaf in Figure 9.1.

Final report

Employing a relatively large final report is the most common approach to project
assessment. The student is expected to undertake the project and submit a report
on their findings and progress. This system works better in conventional colleges
where the student can access the tutor for advice as frequently as required.

Final report
   One assignment, 3–4000 words

Draft assignments
   Outline, non-assessed, 500 words
   Plan of report, non-assessed, 1000 words
   Final report, 5000 words

Independent marking
   Plan, non-assessed, supervisor
   Draft report, 2000 words, supervisor
   Final report, 2000 words, independent marker

Staged
   Two assignments
   Needs
   Goals
   Four assignments
   Outline plan
   Sources used and discarded
   Analysis covering findings
   Report, including lessons learnt

Figure 9.1 *Illustrative examples of approaches to project assessment*

With group projects, students generally split the work of carrying out the project but are each expected to submit separate reports on the project as a whole for assessment. In project credits where the whole course is a project, students often also face a viva much in the same way as they would for a Masters thesis or dissertation.

Draft assignments

In open learning and distance teaching the student normally gets a limited amount of face-to-face support. Here the student benefits from some draft assignment(s) which enables them to check that the topic they have chosen is suitable and that their emphasis is appropriate in the final report.

Typically this is achieved through a short outline describing and justifying the topic selected and a longer draft report which acts as a trial final report. For example, the Open University architecture and design course asked students to submit three pieces of work related to their project: first a non-assessed 500-word outline or statement of intention, then a 1,000-word draft report culminating in a 5,000 word summary report. In project credits a more detailed project plan is also advisable.

Outline and plan

Outlines can be very brief, perhaps just a hundred words. The object of the exercise is to check that the student's topic is appropriate. A plan of the proposed way forward can also be relatively short, say 500 words, but can take the tutor a while to mark. Permitting students to submit a plan in note form rather than polished English may make it easier for them to ask for the advice they need.

Draft

The draft report enables tutors to point out to students if they are presenting something that is some way from what is anticipated. A frequent error is one of emphasis; for example, tutors complained of largely descriptive accounts from OU education students doing a case study project. A note in the course material requesting a description of the subject's background misled some people into devoting half their report to his or her subject's family, social habits and beliefs when a paragraph was intended. In another case, a note asking students to relate the project back to the course was taken by some students to mean a paragraph or so would suffice when something much more substantial had been intended.

Non-assessed

A non-assessed outline and draft report leave students freer to admit the doubts and uncertainties they want advice on. The tutor is then better placed to direct them accordingly. In an assessed plan they feel obliged to present a convincing plan when really they may be confused about what is required and what they intend to do.

Most students do choose to submit these non-assessed outlines and plans (over three-quarters in my OU study). However, a few of the minority who fail to, turn out to be off the mark when they come to submit their final project; since projects often account for a significant proportion of continuous assessment grades this can be a disaster. It can be a good idea to make these non-assessed outlines and draft compulsory to save such students from themselves. If this seems too draconian, Open University experience suggests that merely strongly advising students to submit them increases take-up considerably. This meant three-quarters as opposed to two-thirds of students bothering to submit (Henry, 1978a).

Independent marking

> You knock off a few marks when it's a good point but yours.
> (ODL project tutor)

In conventional teaching it is common to separate the supervisory and marking roles and bring in a second tutor to mark the student's final report. An example of an ODL project course adopting this approach is the Open University ecology course. They allocated students specialist supervisory tutors on the basis of a brief student outline of their intended project. They then required students to submit a more detailed plan to their supervisor. Students were expected to outline how they intended to tackle any anticipated problems. The supervisor commented and the student undertook the project, contacting the supervisor as they needed and sent him or her a 2,000-word draft report of their project. In this case the supervisor actually graded and commented on this report. This gave the student a chance to refine their report. The final version, also 2,000 words, was sent to another tutor with no knowledge of the student. He or she also graded the report.

Sometimes the student supervisor acts as more of a student advocate and merely comments on the student's draft report, with the mark given by an independent tutor. The trouble with this approach is that the course tutor is often aware of all manner of extenuating circumstances to be taken into account when grading – for example, dropping marks for points that the tutor has told the student, giving extra marks when they know the student has produced a good piece of work against the odds.

Staged assignments

The system of staged assignments, where each assignment assesses a different aspect of the project, works well where it is possible to split the project into distinct areas. For example, an undergraduate local history project used four project assignments. In the first assignment, the project *plan*, the student was expected to outline their area of interest and the hypothesis they wished to investigate. In the second assignment on *sources*, the student had to describe the sources he or she had used and those that had been discarded. In the third assignment on *analysis*, the student had to describe the types of analysis they had used, which in this case was often statistical. The last assignment was a *report* on the findings and lessons learned. In this particular case the students were also given the option of combining the first three or the last three assignments, an option few students took, but one which was valued by those who did.

The staged approach seems to be better suited to the weaker student who finds it easier to deal with a project that has to be written up in parts.

Pacing

> Some tutors say get them in by September (late) and they'll be marked. I couldn't do that; I'd be in a big mess in October with masses of work to do. I'd rather be pushed.
> (OU project student)

Both draft and staged assignments have the merit of pacing the student and forcing them to start work.

Weighting

Whatever system is used, teachers may like to consider whether submitting or passing the project should be a compulsory element of the course and whether the project report should be weighted differently to other assignments.

It is common for projects to be designated compulsory. The logic here is that all students should have to tackle similarly demanding work and/or that to merit a pass, students ought to be able to show they can rise to the challenge of project work adequately. However, projects are relatively higher risk activities so this can disadvantage students who end up with little data or face other unforeseen problems.

Project reports generally take longer to prepare than other assignments. Teachers may opt to give them greater weighting in the final assessment to give a better reflection of the time spent. The Open University Personality and Learning Project was weighted as two assignments on these grounds. Many of the students felt a triple weighting would have been more appropriate.

Payment

> I was marking them all summer, you can't skim them as you might an essay.
> (ODL project tutor)

There are good arguments for paying tutors more for marking project assignments than conventional essay assignments, even for an equivalent word length, as project assignments generally take longer to mark, since they are each on different areas. Open University studies suggest tutors regularly spend twice as long or much more time marking projects compared to essays.

Where there are a series of project assignments it is typically the final report that is double-weighted for payment purposes. Of earlier assignments, staged assignments are likely to be paid as other assignments. A short non-assessed outline may receive no extra payment or be combined with a draft outline for the equivalent of a normal assignment payment. Formative preparatory assignments are sometimes relatively brief, say half the length of a conventional assignment, and paid accordingly.

Preparatory assignments

Students doing projects rarely get much training in the skills they will need to undertake their projects. Information and practice in project-related skills such as how to conduct an interview, how to find your way around libraries, formulate hypotheses, analyse and evaluate research and write reports, seem logical prerequisites. Yet students are generally thrown in at the deep end with projects and expected to miraculously acquire the requisite skills as they proceed, a sink or swim philosophy in which the weak can sink. Ideally, students undertaking major projects would complete relevant preparatory assignments much as Ph.D students are now being encouraged to undertake relevant research training.

Across the years

Assignments early in the curriculum can prepare students for the skills they require for project work. For example, the OU government discipline offered a mini-project in an introductory course which involved interviewing and data analysis, and students gratifyingly reported improved confidence in interviewing skills upon completion. They faced a much larger project in the follow-up course in the next year. This course provided extensive written back-up for this larger project in the form of four booklets covering initiating and conducting enquiries, literature searches and compiling a bibliography, writing a report, and examples of reports. Students considered these texts useful but not as useful as actual practice in the skills required would have been.

Within a course

Another tactic is to offer training within a single project course. A successful Open University local history course aimed to provide training in the skills necessary this way. Each of the first four assignments was designed to provide practice in skills needed for the project in later assignments, with assignment one acting as a preparation for assignment five, and two for six, etc. An example is given in Figure 9.2.

Students found the practice in locating, assessing, evaluating and synthesizing data from several sources and writing a report invaluable when they came to do

---

Preparatory assignment

1. Evaluate a research report in the light of course material.
2. Locate and assess the value of some demographic data in the light of a given hypothesis.
3. Test certain hypotheses on two sources of data provided by the course team.
4. Write a report on the strengths and weaknesses of the first part of the course in the light of your reading beyond the course.

Project assignment

5. Justify your project hypothesis and proposed method of enquiry.
6. Assess the value of your project data in the light of your hypothesis.
7. Explain the methods used to exploit your project material.

8. Report on your project findings.

Figure 9.2 *An example of links between preparatory and subsequent assignments*

their own project. However, only very rarely do teachers feel able to allocate so many assignments to train students in this way.

Through formative assignments

> Formative assignment grades and tutor comments really help one to know if one is on the right lines.
> (ODL project student)

> It's an opportunity to test out your ideas with tutor feedback, find out whether you're on the right track and to ask and also to use comments in the final report.
> (ODL project student)

In the case shown in Figure 9.2, all the assignments were summative – that is, they counted towards the student's overall grade. An alternative strategy is to include some formative assignments – that is, assignments that are commented on but where any grade given does not count towards assessment. The fear with offering this kind of assignment is that students will not do it, but formative assignments linked to projects often have a high take-up where students are encouraged to submit them.

The Open University research methods course adopted this approach, offering eight preparatory formative assignments followed by three project assignments.

The first five formative assignments were designed to provide training in skills students would need to undertake the later projects, for example, hypothesis formation and statistical analysis. The last five formative assignments gave the students the opportunity to gain feedback on draft reports for the project assignments. Take-up fell from 90 per cent to 25 per cent and rose again to 75 per cent for the first of the project draft reports. Submission rates appeared to be related to the perceived value of the assignment to the project (Bynner and Henry, 1984; Henry, 1986). The original scheme, shown in Figure 9.3, meant that the assignments that counted were in the latter half of the course; however, an evaluation showed students favoured having some 'money in the bank' earlier. A rescheduling placed the qualitative project earlier and left students much happier. They also favoured fewer assignments, nearer the eight they were used to on a 400-hour course.

Text	Formative assignment	Summative assignment
1. Variety in social science research	1. Trial research report	
2. Beginning research	2a. Hypothesis formulation 2b. Descriptive statistics	
3. Research design	3a. Experimental design or 3b. Evaluate research design	
4. Data collection	4a. Questionnaire design or evaluation 4b. Ethnographic analysis	
5. Classification and measurement	5. Evaluate standardized test	
6. Making sense of data	6. Ethnography project draft	Ethnography project
7. Modelling relationships in data	7. Inferential statistics 8. Survey project draft	Survey project Research evaluation project
8. Evaluation of research		

Figure 9.3 *Research methods material and assignments*

Reaction to the use of formative assignments was mixed. Half the students felt the feedback was valuable:

It gave one an idea how one was progressing and gave the tutor a chance to point out any faults.
(ODL research methods project student)

The assessment strategy was good as it allowed me to get a feel for the course before having to worry about the mark.
(ODL project student)

Though most students did value the unassessed project draft assignments, others had difficulty disciplining themselves to complete unassessed assignments:

They encourage students to be lazy.
(ODL project student)

No real marks for so long left me feeling insecure.
(ODL research methods project student)

They do not provide an incentive to complete unless they carry a small weighting, say 2 per cent.
(ODL project student)

A very low weighting may be enough to encourage many students to complete such assignments.

Marking

Marking projects presents various problems, some of which are listed below, together with suggested remedies:

Pitfalls
- long time to mark
- tendency to reward effort
- few failures
- bi-modal distribution of marks
- own tutor bias.

Ways of improving reliability
- provide assessment criteria
- use double-marking
- run marking standards exercise
- offer feedback on marks
- pay extra.

Grading

Projects often have a different distribution of grades to other assignments. They are failed less often, grades are generally higher on average, and the distribution can be bi-modal rather than normally distributed.

Quality

> I was amazed at the quality, some of them are brilliant.
> (ODL project tutor)

Many students and tutors claim the standard of project work is generally better than normal essay work, so higher grades are to be expected (Henry, 1984; Hodgson and Murphy, 1984). A third of the students in the OU study thought their project work was better than their normal work (Henry, 1977b). The larger and more unstructured the project the greater the percentage of students who felt the work they produced was better than normal. Many students support this assertion, explaining that because they had been given some say in the topic under scrutiny and the way the project was tackled, they felt ownership of the project. Having initiated it they felt more involved, and because they felt more involved they became more motivated and were prepared to put in more hours than they normally would. They also wanted to produce an especially good piece of work to satisfy themselves.

Some students reveal unexpected depths, as projects allow the deep but not quick thinker to show their abilities in a way a three-hour exam fails to:

> One does come across hidden talents.
> (ODL project tutor)

> They're sometimes very clever and don't realize it until they get round to a project where they do much better than their record would lead you to expect.
> (ODL project tutor)

Mace (1975) found higher grades for project than non-project assignments on the same course, ie, 26 per cent grade ones for the project assignments and 8 per cent for the other course assignments. Hodgson and Murphy found the fifth of students who opted to submit the second stage of their biology project achieved higher marks for both parts of the project than those who opted for the safer essay for the second part. One wonders if the project students were more able or had been encouraged to continue after a good first part of their project.

The tendency towards the higher project grading may just apply to larger projects. For example, Melling (1972) found no difference in the distribution of grades awarded on a project exercise and a non-project assignment in the same social science course. On the smaller structured projects studied at the Open University, a greater percentage of students also felt their project work was beneath the standard of work they normally obtain, probably because they were given little responsibility for the design of the project and so felt less involved, and also because these projects asked them to undertake considerably more work than the more usual essay or report assignment and allowed inadequate extra time to do so.

Project prize

The standard of work presented in large projects is often so good that a prize is sometimes offered for the best one submitted. Often this is little more than a public acknowledgement, but sometimes a financial reward has been offered. Samuel (1986) discusses the experience of a $1000 prize for the best engineering design project at the University of Melbourne. The prize was supported by ICI. The intention was to encourage professional attitudes and a greater emphasis on the 'details of construction and ease of manufacture', aspects stressed in the criteria for the award:

> The Award ... is specifically looking for the student(s) with the best engineering potential and will therefore base its assessment on:
>
> *Project concept*
> Originality is desirable, but it should be coupled with an awareness of what is good engineering practice .... .
>
> *Presentation*
> Projects come to fruition by proper communication to many people, so it will be essential that the presentation includes:
> a) A short but complete statement of the engineering essentials of the problem and its proposed solution, in concept and reasonable detail.
> b) Calculations and descriptive notes showing that all significant factors have been considered and that the proposed solution is feasible. Some attention should be given to economic, human and environmental, as well as technical matters.
> c) The final drawings *must* be shown on engineering drawings of acceptable standard. Sketches will *not* be considered adequate, although supplementary freehand three-dimensional views are to be encouraged.
>
> *Teamwork*
> All engineering projects are team efforts, and therefore syndicates should try to form themselves so that individual strengths and weaknesses are

balanced. If practicable, the contribution made by each syndicate member should be stated. It is *not* essential that each member do 'something of everything' (Samuel, 1986, p.219).

Reliability

Academics are often concerned about the reliability of project marking. Concerns centre on how to compare very different products prepared under different circumstances and how to minimize any tutor bias.

Project marker reliability is particularly important as projects often end up counting for a substantial portion of the student's overall grade. For example, Allison and Benson found undergraduate engineering projects generally ended up counting for between 10 and 25 per cent but sometimes as much as 45 per cent (1983, p.402). In architecture courses, projects may account for 100 per cent of the final grade. In open and distance learning the project is often the one compulsory assignment.

Various small studies at the Open University suggest that the reliability of project marking is on a par with that of essay marking and not substantially worse, as some people expect (see, for example, Byrne, 1979; Edwards, 1982; Paton, 1990). For example, in the grading of the project assignments in the ecology course referred to earlier, two-thirds of marks differed by no more than one grade, a difference which compares favourably with the different grades awarded on essay assignments (Murrell, 1975). However, it could be that the use of specialist tutors improved the reliability of the grading on this course. I also have data from two project courses (arts and social science) which double-marked projects and exam questions suggesting project marking is no more unreliable than exam marking.

Ironically, tutors who supervise projects rarely feel grading is a problem. They are generally confident of their ability to mark project reports whether they are submitted in stages or combined. Even where students are given the option of presenting a report of a case study based on supplied materials versus a freely chosen project, OU tutors have felt able to compare these different assignments adequately. Their one complaint is usually that project reports take a long time to mark and they should be paid extra for doing so (Henry, 1978a; Paton, 1990).

Comparison

The usual method tutors use to help determine the relative marks they are awarding is to *compare* many different assignments. Ironically, in project work tutors are sometimes allocated less students to allow extra time to be spent with each. Having fewer projects to compare can make marking harder.

One can also ask all tutors to mark the same project(s), an exercise designed to aid the development of a common standard. A number of authors feel that obliging tutors to grade projects on a scheme along the lines of that outlined in Table 9.1 helps to standardize marks.

Own tutor effect

> It is difficult balancing achievement against effort when one's had a lot of contact with the students.
> (ODL project tutor)

A commonly expressed fear is that project supervisors may be reluctant to fail projects. Edwards (1979) undertook a study of project assessment partly aimed at determining whether or not course supervisors were more generous markers than independent assessors. She found a small difference, with tutors grading their own students' projects about half a grade higher than the independent markers. Allison and Benson also (1983) allude to this problem. Some of this discrepancy may be accounted for by the students' own tutors' greater knowledge of the difficulties they faced in undertaking the project.

I found that tutors new to projects can find it particularly difficult to separate supervisory and assessment roles. The students' own supervisor will sometimes admit to a tendency to mark for effort and a reluctance to fail students who have put in a lot of extra time (Henry, 1977a).

Interestingly, the OU study suggests that students do not feel their tutors are particularly generous markers when it comes to projects. While a half were satisfied with the grade awarded, more of the remainder felt the tutor had graded them severely than leniently. This concern was more apparent in the smaller than larger unstructured and structured project exercises (Henry, 1978a).

Tutor bias

Some reviewers have been worried that markers' value judgements get in the way of the grade awarded – a problem which is by no means unique to projects. For example, after an examination of 100 project assignments, Bates (1976) felt some social science tutors had marked down students for doing what they ought to do, because they were unsympathetic to a quantitative approach. After scrutinizing discrepancies between tutors' project marks in some detail, staff responsible for the OU research methods course concluded that at least part of the differences could be accounted for by a few different methodological preferences, for example on appropriate ways of using statistics. Tutor notes making explicit the methods the course authors deemed acceptable appeared to minimize the level of future discrepancy (Henry, 1984).

Assessment criteria

It's how they've gone about it that counts, not what they've found out.
(ODL project tutor)

You read through and apply the usual standards, throw in your judgement, trying to make some assessment of what they have done. Have they used it in a simple-minded way, just lifted it with a few amendments? In which case a bare pass. The quality of style and paragraphs that follow each other are important.
(ODL project tutor)

A bare pass is invariably regurgitation of bits of insights lifted straight from the course or that you've fed them. A 2 has some flashes of intuition and it's nicely laid out. A 2.1 makes points you don't get unless you've thought hard, relating two books together. A first usually involves work on a subject that is difficult material, that is not easily used. It shows flashes of invention and clever handling. Where they've got no statistics on a subject, producing something as a near substitute. They are sophisticated in terms of argument.
(ODL project tutor)

Tutors claim the criteria they use to grade projects are similar to those they would use for essays or reports; for example, relevance to the question originally posed, support for arguments, comprehensiveness, coherent format, logical reasoning, succinctness, originality, etc.

Often a portion of marks is left for the way the student has tackled the project and a portion for the analysis of the findings and the final outcome. It is extremely important that tutors mark the process – the way the student has conducted the project, not the product – whether or not he or she achieved a positive or negative outcome, so students who failed to get a desirable outcome through no fault of their own are not penalized.

In unstructured projects it is often very difficult to specify assessment criteria in detail and it is common to rely fairly heavily on the skill and expertise of the teacher. Often criteria relating to general skills and abilities are used; for example, justification for project choice, hypothesis formulation, clarity of aims, links with course material, evidence to back-up conclusions, analysis of results and clear presentation.

It is sometimes claimed that simple marking guidelines can help minimize the discrepancy in marks awarded between different project types, eg, computer projects and design and construct type projects, and between the students who successfully completed their project and those who did not. In the context of engineering projects, Jackson (1987) suggests that marking uncertainties arise when the student is too dependent on his or her supervisor or meets problems with scarcity of information, apparatus or components. Table 9.1 illustrates Jackson's suggested guidelines.

Table 9.1 *Engineering project assessment form*

	%
Assessment of project work	
1. Appreciation and approach to project, competence in planning	10
2. Originality, innovation, development of ideas	15
3. Practical skill in experimental or theoretical work	15
4. Extent of achieving objectives, success in overcoming difficulties	10
Report presentation	
1. Overall planning, logical development, readability	10
2. Quality of language, diagrams, freedom from errors	10
3. Clarity of introductory review and conclusions	10
Assessment of initiative	
1. Diligence, initiative, application, and supervision required	10
2. Amount of extra reading, library research	10
Total	100

Source: Jackson (1987).

Double-marking

> Double-marking gives you a clearer guide to the standard of your work.
> (ODL project student)

> It gives you a second chance if you are not hitting it off with your tutor.
> (ODL project student)

Double-marking is used more commonly on projects than other assignments largely because project work entails a major independent piece of work. For example, Allison and Benson (1983) found that 92 per cent of the 60 institutions included in their survey of undergraduate engineering projects used two markers to assess projects. The use of double-marking is designed to give the student a better chance of a fair grade; it also acts as a welcome check on any unreliability in the student's own supervisor, counteracting any tendency he or she might have to be unduly generous or biased against the student's work. There is no doubt there is a lot to be said for double-marking any large project. However, double-marking means double payment and is sometimes dropped because of the expense and extra work involved.

Blind double-marking

> It helps alleviate students' fears that their tutor is a hard marker.
> (ODL project tutor)

> It gave me a greater measure of confidence in the results.
> (ODL project tutor)

When the project student receives a mark for the final report from both their supervisor and an independent tutor, the 'independent' second marker is often made aware of the supervisor's grade. This knowledge is likely to affect the grade awarded and ideally double-marking should be blind. However, I realize this is a counsel of excellence rarely achieved in conventional education, never mind ODL.

The OU research methods course did double-mark their projects blind for several years. An evaluation (Henry, 1986) showed students and tutors felt double-marking to be particularly necessary where the student's grade would result in marks for only a few pieces of work, say marks for three project assignments versus eight essays. There was also some support for the fairness of a second 'objective' mark by a tutor who was not supervising the student and a belief that the student's own tutor would mark more thoroughly because the project was to be marked by another person.

Of course students who receive discrepant marks are generally less happy:

> There was a wide gap between the two marks which suggests each emphasize different criteria.
> (ODL project student)

Sometimes where tutors disagree over the appropriate way forward for a particular project, blind double-marking can be problematic:

> Suggestions made by my tutor on the draft report were followed. This resulted in a higher grade from my own tutor but the approach was severely criticized by the second tutor, with a lower grade given.
> (ODL project student)

Where grades differ some kind of arbitration procedure is appropriate. The OU research methods projects which were double-marked averaged differences of a grade. They re-marked any assignment where the grade difference was two or more, ie, 2.1 to a 3. There is also a case for re-marking any discrepancies between pass and fail and those achieving a distinction or not. I found tutors thought it fair to average discrepancies of 1 or 2 grades (ie, 1st to 2.1 or 2.2) when double-marking several project-based assignments in a mass distance education system, but that 3 or 4 grade differences (ie, 1st to 3rd) should always be referred to a third party for a re-mark (Henry, 1986).

In order to avoid any difficulties with discrepant grades, tutors may consider a system whereby they both mark the project, preferably blind, then agree a common grade to present to the student. However, when I asked open learning students and tutors if they would prefer projects to be double-marked blind or discussed by two tutors who presented a single grade, both favoured blind double-marking, the students presumably because they could see any discrepancies and appeal to a third party, the tutors due to pragmatic difficulties and the time and expense needed to discuss grades over the phone (Henry, 1986).

Exams

Most projects are assessed through presentations, reports or some other form of continuous assessment. Exams are generally considered an inappropriate way of assessing this kind of work. A written exam would not be an appropriate means of assessing a project credit, for example. Where no exam is employed, some independent check on the supervisor's grading and the student's ability is often considered necessary. This may take the form of a viva, independent assessment or double-marking, and helps counteract any charge that the student might have cheated.

However, in some situations, for instance where the proportion of continuous assessment to exam work is fixed, students are asked about their project work in an exam. The use of exam questions on projects is almost invariably in addition to continuous assessment of the project. Exams are far from ideal places to assess project work, but staff have been pretty creative with their questions.

Mostly the exam questions ask the student variants on the following:

- What have you learnt from undertaking the project?
- What further research would you wish to take to follow up this work?
- How would you tackle your project differently now, if you knew then what you do now?

Many students find these kinds of questions no more or less difficult than other exam questions. Indeed I found students who thought exam questions on projects were less worrying because doing the project meant it was easier to remember what you had done than with other material.

In open and distance learning situations, project exam questions can be used as a cheaper method of providing a second opinion of the student's project than paying a double-marker to assess a long project report. Vivas may then be used where the student's continuous assessment and exam grade are very different.

Review

Project assignments are often compulsory, either because staff feel they offer a suitably demanding task for students to be assessed on, or to ensure equity of effort because projects are generally deemed to be more difficult than other assignments. Project work may be assessed in stages or by a final report. In the latter case, progress is more satisfactory if a brief non-assessed outline and draft project report are included.

There is some evidence that the reliability of project marking is on a par with that for essays, not worse. There is also some evidence that course supervisors grade projects slightly higher than independent markers. In an ideal world all major projects would be double-marked.

Points for reflection

How many assignments would you use to assess a project?
Would any of these be non-assessed?
What word length would you ask for? Would this include appendices or not?
What proportion of continuous assessment would you allocate to the project?
Would you make the project compulsory?
How would you improve marker reliability?
If you were to ask an exam question on the project what would it be?

Chapter 10

Tuition

A good tutor makes you feel you can do it.
(ODL project student)

Students undertaking project work are expected to make greater demands on a tutor than when studying conventionally. I found that contact with the tutor through telephone, correspondence and class tutorials was higher on project courses than non-project courses and the level of satisfaction with the help received was also higher, especially on the unstructured (larger and more open-ended) projects (Henry, 1978a).

Yet open and distance learning often provides less face-to-face tuition than in conventional education. Since unstructured projects are often supported by less material than the average ODL course, any savings in material preparation could be used to offset the extra cost of providing more tuition (Henry, 1989b). Indeed, where project courses, such as project credits, attract low student numbers it can be cheaper to support students via a tutor than going to the expense of preparing high cost distance learning materials that need high student numbers to offset the capital-intensive start-up costs (Henry, 1993). Nevertheless, the question remains as to how the educator is to make best use of the limited amount of tuition they have available and whether it is sufficient to supervise and assist students studying projects adequately, especially where they are studying at a distance.

Demand

Though projects are expected to make fairly heavy demands on a tutor, individual students vary considerably in the amount of help they need. Most students need more help than normal; a few become extremely demanding, making noticeable inroads on a tutor's time; and a minority do not need help. For example, the OU study found that whereas three-quarters of students felt they needed to contact their tutor to discuss the project, a quarter did not. The percentage wanting help varied with the size of project, from an average of over 90 per cent on the largest unstructured project to nearer a half on the smallest structured project. Between 30 per cent and virtually 100 per cent of students contacted their tutor about their project, the higher percentage applying to the larger projects. Students on the largest unstructured projects also valued tutor help most highly. On average, about 70 per cent of students found their tutor helpful but half the students doing unstructured projects found their tutor very helpful compared to only a quarter undertaking structured projects (Henry, 1978a).

On average, a fifth of students in the unstructured project sample did not feel the need for any more assistance over and above the minimal amount provided, compared to about a third of students studying structured projects. It may be that the percentage of students who prefer to get on with the project themselves and do not need help from their tutor is higher than normal because self-sufficient students are more likely to be attracted to ODL in general and projects in particular.

Where the project is just one component within a course, one finds that students studying the open-ended projects want extra tutor help more for their project work than with the other course material. My study found half the students studying unstructured projects wanted more tutor help specifically for the project compared to under a twentieth wanting help with course work, even where the latter was meant to take up the bulk of the students' time. On the smaller structured projects, the majority wanted help with both. Cross and Ransome (1977) also report a demand for more tutorial help for their unstructured project.

Lower student ratio

Project credits, where the whole course is a project, are expected to make especially large demands on the tutor. Special arrangements are often made, allocating tutors on such courses a low student:tutor ratio. For example, the School for Independent Study at the University of East London allocated one central studies tutor per 11 students. The Open University has reduced the ratio from one to 20 or 25 to one to five or less in some cases. Often students and tutors are personally matched according to the student's area of interest.

In such situations the importance of the relationship with the tutor can be critical – '…you're working so closely with one lecturer that if there is poor rapport you are in a really bad situation for four terms', (from University of London School for Independent Study, in Percy and Ramsden, 1980). A large percentage of students (though not all) need a good working relationship with their tutor and want to meet periodically for social as much as pedagogic reasons: 'there must be a close personal relationship; the director of study must be really interested in the student's work and through working together a bond grows between them' (ibid.).

The need for guidance

> Adults need lots of psychological support and lots of tutorials. If you let them loose on a project they like everything to be perfect. They worry if they have deficient data, seeing it as a personal failure and you have to reassure them that this isn't so and the value is in setting out and doing it on their own.
> (OU project tutor)

In open learning situations as elsewhere, much of the support a student requires during a project is psychological.

My studies suggest open learning project students usually need help at three main points: when choosing the topic, during data collection, and while writing up, for reasons elaborated in Chapters 4 to 6 and summarized below. The amount of help wanted at each stage seems to vary with the type of project.

Choosing a topic

> There are a lot of people who want reassurance early on.
> (ODL project tutor)

> A major problem is getting them started, once they've formulated an outline they feel morally committed to the idea.
> (ODL project tutor)

> In the first year I didn't like to dampen their enthusiasm. Mind you I'm quite firm now, ruling out anything I think won't work, if they'll take my advice.
> (ODL project tutor)

> Supervisors should tread fairly carefully, they don't want to let rubbish go through, but on the other hand their role in telling the student what to do is a difficult one; they can't write the thesis for the student ... for an undergraduate one has no misgivings about identifying the weak spot.
> (ODL project tutor)

The first stage often causes the most problems for tutors. An early meeting with the student gives the tutor a chance to explain what is involved, and indicate the expected scope, hopefully changing any general anxieties to actionable ones in the process. The tutor is also well advised to emphasize the merits of picking a project that is feasible rather than basing the selection solely on interest. New tutors are often reluctant to give too much firm advice, though as they get more experienced they tend to be more forthcoming.

On project credits, tutors can find it problematic to decide to what extent it is appropriate for them to help the student restructure their project. Percy and Ramsden (1980) point out that drawing the line between giving help and allowing initiative can be especially problematic in institutions, such as the School for Independent Study, that espouse an educational philosophy emphasizing student independence.

Collecting information

> Often they drift in the early months, they don't realize the urgency and it needs pointing out.
> (ODL project tutor)

> They regularly underestimate the number of visits they'll need.
> (ODL project tutor)

> They don't appreciate they are going to pursue blind alleys unwittingly.
> (ODL project tutor)

It is helpful if the tutor forewarns students new to project work of the problems they are likely to experience, but will not anticipate, as this can help to curtail downheartedness which easily strikes the lone researcher who doesn't realize that set-backs are part of the territory.

It is also important to encourage students to start looking for information as early as possible to allow for any unexpected eventualities.

The tutor is likely to get asked about likely sources of information. Since much of this information is standard, tutors may like to consider presenting it in print form.

Analysing and writing up

> I only saw my tutor once and he so demoralized me. I'd done all this work on non-conformists and their voting behaviour (good point for me I thought and for all my hard work) and he more or less cut me down flat. It put me off for four weeks and I didn't see him again.
> (ODL project student)

Students are often very sensitive about their projects and tutors need to be particularly diplomatic.

It is worth reiterating the need to allow ample time for analysing and writing up, the major points expected, as well as the form and style of the report, and details of any assessment criteria.

Training

Where the tutorial provision is more generous, group tutorials can be used to offer training in the skills required for the project. For example, the OU Research Methods course team suggested five three- to five-hour activities suitable for group meetings between the tutor and their students, giving students the opportunity to do research as well as learn about it from the outset:

1 Computer induction and practice in generating data for formative trial report assignment
2 Conducting a piece of experimental research
3 Practice in survey and ethnographic interviewing
4 Help with project work analysis including use of the computer
5 Help with final evaluation project.

The OU is very careful to offer these kind of activities as suggestions only, so tutors who feel they have a better plan are free to try it. In practice we find that far from resenting such suggestions, most tutors are grateful and go on to use the activities during their tutorials with students. If staff are encouraged to write in with further suggestions these can easily be expanded, amended and refined over the years.

Ways of providing tutor support

Face-to-face support

It is generally assumed that some form of face-to-face support is a prerequisite for students to undertake projects successfully, and there is no doubt that some face-to-face support helps. I found over a fifth of my OU sample wanted more face-to-face support to discuss their project whereas under a tenth wanted this help to assist with their course work.

Tutorials

Attendance at project tutorials is normally higher than usual. Most students feel the need for some extra support, particularly if the project is a large unstructured piece of work. For example, Thorpe (1977) presents data which show attendance at tutorials on courses with projects compared to those without. In education, technology and science faculties it was the courses including projects that had the highest percentage of students attending tutorials. I also found that a slightly higher percentage of students who finished their project work had discussed their project face-to-face with their tutor (Henry, 1978b, p.116–18).

The amount of support offered can be limited if it is offered at appropriate times. For example, most Open University students only attend two or three group tutorials when undertaking a project of anything from 30 to 100-odd hours (though they are free to telephone or write to their tutor).

Tutorial provision

Most ODL students find projects much easier if they have the option of at least some face-to-face help at key points. My studies suggest that a minimum of three face-to-face tutorials are sufficient for many ODL project components provided they are placed at appropriate points, ie, just before the student has to decide on a topic, during collecting information and towards the end of analysis. Figure 10.1 summarizes when to schedule and what points to deal with where tutorial support is at a premium. On an Open University course involving around 200 hours study time which incorporates a 50-hour project, each tutor might be allocated something something like 12 to 25 hours tuition for 20 students. Three two- to five-hour face-to-face sessions may be set aside to deal with the project.

Tutorial	Stage	Areas to cover
First	Pre-choosing topic	Relieve anxiety Indicate scope
Second	While collecting data	Discuss local sources of information
Third	During analysis and writing up	Offer individual help on students' data while students share problems

Figure 10.1 *Optimum use of limited face-to-face contact for project work*

Group versus individualized help

Because projects are on different areas, brief individual help can often be more effective than group discussions. However, tuition is an expensive resource and where tutor time is limited the dilemma is sometimes whether to hold a group discussion or offer private help. Students undertaking substantial projects generally find individual help more useful than group tutorials. (For example half the students in the OU study found individual assistance very helpful compared to a quarter describing group tutorials as very helpful. Two-fifths of the unstructured students also wanted extra individual help at group tutorials compared to 6 per cent wanting more group discussion.)

The larger and more unstructured the project, the greater the demand for individualized help from the tutor and the less point in any group discussion. However, with medium-sized project components of around 50 to 100 hours duration, there is something to be said for combining the two approaches, offering group tutorials with some time set aside for individual advice. Five or ten minutes individual advice is often sufficient for a tutor to solve many student queries. In group settings, students can talk among themselves, learning what each other is doing, reassuring themselves that others have similar problems and helping with information on sources, while the tutor deals with individual problems.

Voluntary groups

In some situations any tutorial provision may seem too expensive. In these circumstances it is sometimes possible to use volunteer facilitators to assist. For example, the Open University community education department has linked up with various voluntary networks, such as the Pre-school Playgroups Association, volunteers from which have facilitated groups of students studying the OU parenting courses.

Self-help groups

> We go through the standard assignments but there's not much you can do
> on projects because they are all so different.
> (OU student)

Alternatively, peer-led self-help groups can provide substitute support for students. Staff can help their formation by circulating each student's name to the other students in the course. Note that the Data Protection Act means that students must agree to releasing their names, addresses and telephone numbers before these are circulated.

One might fear, as the quote above implies, that self-help groups would offer little for students working on different topics (as they often are in project work) but it seems not. Something between a fifth and third of Open University students studying project courses do have regular contact with their fellows. Furthermore, over three-quarters found this helpful for their project (Henry, 1978a). Few however wanted any more assistance from their fellows, except a minority of those undertaking social research projects.

Mentors

Another strategy is to use some kind of mentor, for example to pair each project student with a student who completed the project the previous year. Similarly, new tutors can be given the name of a tutor who is an experienced project tutor. In 'real world' projects students are often given a 'mentor' from the organization in which they are completing a project as well as an academic tutor.

No face-to-face tuition

> It strikes me that distance tuition is more possible with project work. After all, this is how one supervises research students. They send in chapters and you send back comments all over them.
> (ODL project tutor)

In much of the discussion above we have assumed a project is an activity that is carried out under supervision. In considering whether or not such support is really necessary it is perhaps worth remembering that individuals undertake a lot of unsupervised learning. According to Tough's research on independent learning projects (which was undertaken in nine countries including Australia, Israel, the UK and Zaire), adults spend about 500 hours a year on average on five major learning efforts. Three-quarters of these are planned by the learner and only a fifth take place under the guidance of a professional educator or through distance study (Tough, 1985).

Distance educators have offered projects with no tuition at all or no face-to-face tuition. For example, Open University ecology and statistics courses have offerred projects without any face-to-face tuition and, while this is not ideal, it has worked adequately. However, project tutors report difficulties on trying to advise students on data analysis at a distance, for example what to do with a poll book or rock they cannot see.

In the ecology course, students were also allocated specialist tutors who lived some distance away from them. Many opted to write rather than telephone their tutor. Perhaps the success of the distance taught project is not so surprising as it mirrors the situation in which postgraduates often find themselves.

Residential school

One way round the problem of offering projects at a distance is to reserve them for periods when the students come together with a tutor, for example at a residential school. At the Open University, several courses have used this option and scheduled project activities over a short period of residential tuition (normally a week or weekend). Several of the psychology residentials are largely based round projects, and the ecology course decided to devote the whole of their school to helping students with their project. Perhaps more common is the model where one or two sessions are set aside to offer general assistance and answer specific queries.

Face-to-face support is so valued that several OU project courses have offered students the option of a voluntary weekend school specifically to assist their project work where none has been provided by the institution. Despite the fact that this is a self-financed exercise which students have to pay for over and above their normal course fee, something like 80 per cent of students undertaking the research methods project course, for example, were willing to give up a weekend, travel many miles and pay for the privilege to attend.

Use of telephone and correspondence tuition

The range is once or twice to a weekly letter or telephone conversation.
(OU project tutor)

Often you get one or two who are obsessive and it's an hour's phone call quieting their nerves rather than giving information.
(OU project tutor)

Some people prefer not to be face-to-face, actually seeing your supervisor. The project is your baby and you don't want your baby criticized, whereas in a letter they'll think about your amendments.
(ODL project tutor)

You'll get a student ring and say, 'I've come across a minute book, what can I do with it?' What can I do without looking at it? I don't know the poor law of Stanmore.
(ODL project tutor)

In open learning situations, where specialized projects are employed and the student is geographically or socially isolated, some form of communication other than face-to-face tuition may be necessary. Some students actually prefer this kind of distant contact even it can be difficult to advise on what to do with certain kinds of data without face-to-face contact.

Tutors can expect to receive more calls from students on project courses than non-project-based courses, though individuals vary widely in the amount of help they require. Often the assistance given is more a matter of psychological support.

Most people seem to find the telephone a more conducive medium than letter for many of the things they wish to ask about. Feedback suggests that both modes of advice are valued on any sizeable project. In the OU study, four-fifths of students wrote at least one letter and a half telephoned their tutor, and 70 per cent of students doing unstructured and semi-structured courses rated their tutors' comments as helpful. About half the students felt the need to contact their tutor more about their project than course work by telephone on the unstructured projects compared to a quarter of those doing structured projects.

Generally it's 'Can I do x, y or z?' To which the answer is invariably 'Yes'.
(ODL project student)

It's so frustrating when things go wrong, that's why you need a tutor to say, 'Don't be frustrated'.
(ODL project student)

Tutor contact

Unfortunately in many projects a large minority of students do not feel able to contact their tutor as much as they would wish. This can range from about a third to a half of the students. When I asked the reason for this timidity, I found that the most commonly volunteered reason is a reluctance to bother the tutor. Other reasons included difficulty contacting the supervisor, that they were unhelpful or not very knowledgeable (Henry, 1978a). Some tutors make it clear they do not wish to be troubled by students, by sounding irritated on the phone, putting off or curtailing meetings, appearing distracted, etc. The vast majority are happy for students to contact them.

One way of encouraging tutor contact is to set aside a particular day of the week for project queries. Tutors felt that expecting students to wait six days was no bad thing, as they might sort out minor queries themselves in the interim.

The tutor's role

By allowing the student more freedom to organize their own learning, project work also places more responsibility on the tutor. This enhanced role is often welcomed by tutors, despite the fact that projects normally take longer to supervise than essays and other course work. Indeed some tutors prefer facilitating and supervising project courses to the more predictable lecture or materials-based course. Such tutors find project work more stimulating and speak of the satisfaction in knowing you have 'fed the right stuff in at the right time'.

ODL pre-packaged modules predetermine the curriculum and do much of the teaching for the tutor. Some staff welcome this as it makes their life easier, but many other tutors are frustrated with the limited role offered them in much open learning and distance teaching situations and welcome the extra responsibility implicit in project work. They enjoy the additional freedom involved in tutoring projects. Thus project work can help maintain the interest of the tutors.

Some converts to open learning point out that it enables them to abolish lectures by substituting distance learning packages and reserving all their time to act as a facilitator helping students with project- and portfolio-based learning.

Specialist tutors

On the whole, most school and many college and university projects can be supervised satisfactorily by any tutor in the relevant discipline, and this system seems to work adequately. Specialized theses and dissertations, such as project credits – where the whole course is a project – are normally taught by specialist tutors whose interests and specialisms are appropriate for the students' proposed area. Tutors nearly always feel perfectly competent to facilitate projects on a wide variety of areas at school or undergraduate level. Students, however, are not always so sure – a third to a fifth of the OU project students claimed they would have preferred a specialist tutor even if that meant losing the option of face-to-face tuition and having to correspond by letter.

Sometimes it is considered appropriate to match project topics to specialized supervisors at the outset, for instance to ensure that the botanist looks after the botany projects and the zoologist the zoology projects. This may be necessary if one area has undergone recent advances non-specialists may not be aware of. For example, OU hard rock geologists have found it difficult to supervise the soft rock projects; allocation of projects to specialists at the outset avoids such problems.

Tutors often welcome a list of their fellow tutors' specialisms, so tutors can help each other when faced with a project-area they are unfamiliar with.

Payment

There is a good case for paying tutors more for supervising projects than normal course work. For example, Open University tutors reckoned it took them one to two hours to mark each 3,000-word project assignment, with a survey project taking longer and a research paper evaluation project the least time (Henry, 1984). Since the topic areas are all different, and projects are more demanding and time-consuming, there is increased student/tutor contact and invariably additional marking time required. Some tutors are willing to undertake this work because they find it more stimulating and rewarding and do not begrudge the additional time needed. However, as the novelty may wear off and projects benefit from high quality tuition, extra payment is worth considering.

Some institutions pay double for marking project assignments to allow for the extra time needed to mark assignments on different areas. Many others do not. With project credits – the larger thesis or dissertation-like projects – the tutor may be given a smaller number of students to supervise and/or be paid on a higher rate that takes account of anticipated extra demands on the tutor's time.

Cost

Some more extensive projects make much greater demands on the tutor's time. For example, in curricula which are more student-driven, staff may rely on the use of individually negotiated learning contracts to determine the content of the course the student will follow. Project credits where the whole course is a project also typically require one-to-one negotiation between tutor and student. The trouble with this level of support is that it is much harder to offer in open and distance learning where staff and learners are geographically distant from one another. The cost of providing individual support for a project is also sometimes seen as a factor limiting take-up.

Another strategy is to cover as much of the advice as possible in learning materials, obviating the need for so much tutor time. For example, Lupton (1976) devised a generalized contract which he terms 'the project syllabus method' as a way of offering the flexibility inherent in an individual learning contract at much less cost. Essentially this comprised a mass-produced contract and back-up materials describing the objectives, resources, possible topical enquiries, grading procedures and expected report format, plus ways of beginning the enquiry suitable for a wide variety of field projects. The document suggests many possible options and permits students to substitute their own. For example, the Community Interaction project syllabus covered business, education, crime, politics and local government, architecture and local planning, pollution, transport, public work, issues and attitudes in the community, health, recreation and conservation. Students were expected to undertake a series of mini-projects in these areas. The more specialized Law and Society project syllabus offered quite specific advice. For example, in a project concerning bail-bonding, the following questions were used as prompts: 'How does it work, how is it controlled, who is involved in it, what do they get out of it, what happens when bail is broken, legal problems related thereto, bail for the poor, who is concerned about problems if there are problems?' Associated reading gave relevant agencies who may assist the enquiry, such as non-profit legal advisory services, police, court officials, social workers, rehabilitation and advocacy groups, plus a recommended text. The fairly large numbers of students using this system (over 1,000) presumably justified the preparation work involved.

Review

The role of the tutor in project work is more important than in normal course work, the more so the larger and more unstructured the project. Students on such projects feel they need and value the tutor's help more than those on smaller structured projects. The majority of students want more tuition for project work than other course work, especially on unstructured projects.

Those contemplating a project as part of an open learning programme would be well advised to set aside at least three occasions when the student meets the tutor to discuss the project, ideally prior to topic selection, during data collection and in the period of analysis and writing up the project report. Group tutorials on project work are often more efficient if the tutor spends some time seeing students individually while the other participants talk amongst themselves.

Tutors faced with students who are reluctant to bother them can go a long way towards overcoming this simply by emphasizing that calls are expected and setting aside periods when such help would be available.

Points for reflection

Will you offer projects face-to-face or at a distance? Will you use general or specialist tutors?

How many hours tuition will you allocate for project work? How much, if any, of this will be face-to-face?

What other media would you expect to use – telephone, audio, letter, conferencing, fax?

Can you schedule a tutorial at the outset, during data collection, and during writing up?

Can you circulate each student's name and address and telephone number to the other students?

Can you circulate information on tutors' specialisms to other tutors?

Could tutors be asked to produce or update guidance on the project and guidelines on local sources of information?

Can you pay tutors extra for marking project assignments?

Will you reduce the number of students that tutors supervise on project credits?

Chapter 11

Outcomes

> It would be more valuable to pursue fewer projects in greater depth.
> (ODL project student)

Students find project work difficult, but it is partly the challenge of overcoming difficulties for themselves that students respond to, and which leads them to value the experience highly. The OU study showed that though a high percentage have difficulties on large projects, such projects are among the most popular in terms of the percentage of students finding them very interesting and worthwhile, whereas the least challenging smaller projects had the lowest percentage having difficulties and the lowest percentages finding the project interesting or worthwhile. Response to open and distance learning projects has been just as enthusiastic as in conventional teaching situations (see, for example, Cross and Ransome, 1977; Henry, 1978a, 1984, 1986, 1992; Mace, 1975; Paton and Lay, 1986; Spear, 1977; Varley, 1975).

Value

> The project was the highlight of the course for me.
> (OU student)

> The project was the most enjoyable and rewarding part of the course.
> (OU student)

> The project is interesting and carries over better to your own organization; when you focus on one specific point, you start thinking critically about all the things you do.
> (ODL management student)

Projects generate a tremendous amount of interest in the majority of students who generally judge this type of activity worthwhile, useful and relevant. Generally over four-fifths of students in OU studies have found their project work interesting and worthwhile. However, the degree of perceived value relates very closely to the amount of freedom given the student and size of the enterprise – more freedom breeds greater satisfaction. Unstructured projects produce a much more positive response than structured projects. Kroll (1985) reports a similarly positive response in respect of laboratory projects, with up to three-quarters of students preferring these to regular labs and over three-quarters enjoying the project.

The percentage of students rating the outcome of undertaking a project highly increases directly with the lack of structure and size of the project (see Table 11.1). On large projects where the student is given considerable freedom, I found over four-fifths of students may be expected to find the work very interesting, worthwhile and useful, which is a far cry from the typical response to educational endeavours. On the smaller unstructured projects, around two-thirds described their projects as very interesting, worthwhile and useful. On structured projects that provided options, about half found the work very interesting, worthwhile and useful and about a quarter did so on the structured projects with set topics. Here, however, about a third of students felt that work they had undertaken for the smallest projects was not worthwhile. Sunderland and Toncheva (1991) also found over half their students thought the project the most useful part of their English language course.

A slightly different picture emerges when we look at the relevance of the project work to the rest of the course. Projects are often not well integrated, with course work. Where they are integrated students tend to appreciate them more.

Table 11.1 *Students' ratings of projects*

	Larger unstructured	*Smaller unstructured*	*Semi-structured*	*Structured*
	%	%	%	%
Very interesting	90	70	55	35
Very worthwhile	80	55	45	25
Very useful	80	70	50	25
Very relevant	50	50	50	50

Source: Adapted from Henry (1978b)

Rewards

> You get a sense of satisfaction, of personal achievement you don't get after reading course material and writing assignments on it.
> (ODL project student)

> You attain a level you've not attained before, you feel you've achieved something, something of your own.
> (ODL project student)

> The non-academic rewards are important – they feel they have achieved a level they have not achieved before – something of their own.
> (ODL project tutor)

> It's in the nature of a project you can't turn to secondary materials, so you have to think things out for yourself – a real stimulus towards thought.
> (ODL project student)

I found many students on unstructured projects were positively ecstatic about the delights of projects, a point recognized by tutors: 'The vast majority become enthralled'. Many students undertaking large unstructured projects talk about their project work as the most important aspect of their academic work. I also found enthusiastic students even on the structured projects. Fail (1991) paints a similar picture:

> As time went on, I found that we began to act as a scientific team: re-evaluating goals and experimental design, interpreting data, figuring out next moves and so on. As students were routinely treated as scientific colleagues they developed confidence in their scientific abilities and an amazingly intense desire to see their projects come to a successful conclusion.

There are several factors that accounted for the enthusiasm I encountered. First, students welcomed the challenge and responsibility involved in doing a large independent piece of work, based on the world outside. Second, they welcomed the opportunity of following an interest of their own. Because they had chosen the topic and located, selected, analysed and organized the material themselves, they developed a personal pride in the work that they did not feel for an ordinary assignment, and since the task is far from easy, they felt a terrific sense of satisfaction at having produced their own project. Students also felt that they had learnt a lot through doing a project and were convinced of the merit of having to sort out material first-hand rather than having someone do that stage for them as is usually the case in so much education.

We get a clearer picture of the reasons for the very rewarding nature of project work when we look at the most commonly valued attributes. Project work can enable learners to get into a subject deeply and get a better understanding of the difficulties in research and methodological shortcomings, relate theory to practice, and improve their ability to synthesize information from various sources. My research (Henry, 1978a) indicates that it is the challenge of project work to which students respond. Common outcomes included:

- Having to use initiative
- Following my own interests
- Getting into a subject deeply
- Working independently
- Gaining first-hand experience
- Having to work things out for myself
- Being stretched intellectually
- Producing something of my own
- Learning to do things I've not done before.

I also found that, excepting 'first-hand experience' and 'doing things not done before', students on unstructured projects mentioned these attributes more frequently than those on structured projects. Not surprisingly, students who finished the project also mentioned more positive attributes than those who had not (Henry, 1978a).

In the OU study, nearly all projects were judged to have provided insights into research and helped students relate theory to practice, but it was unstructured projects, especially the larger ones, that were more likely to be rated as enabling students to get into the subject deeply and learn a lot about the subject, stimulate an enduring interest and improve their ability to synthesize information. The larger unstructured projects also had the highest percentage who felt they had been stretched intellectually.

The list above does not adequately convey the depth of enthusiasm many students felt for the project work. Many students, especially those on large projects, talk of a great sense of achievement. Many writers (for example, Henry, 1989a; Kennedy, 1982; Sunderland and Toncheva, 1991) also talk of the increased confidence noticeable in students after they have completed a project. The practical experience of undertaking a project also helps ground related course material.

Value to the community

Many projects are of such a high standard that they provide a valuable source of information in their own right. For example, the OU architecture and design projects were considered such an important source of data on the history of buildings that a national archive of these projects was set up at the Royal Institute of British Architects. The course team reckon that 10 per cent of student projects on this course made a strikingly original contribution (Mace, 1984). The science foundation course mini-project discovered several new species of fruit-fly over the years it ran. The research methods project on class provides 15 years of national data on changing attitudes to class. The environmental health course provided useful regional data on pollution.

Clearly there is potential here for teachers to use students to collect data for their own pet projects. My research unearthed only one project where students had a slight feeling of resentment, as though they had been used as cheap labour, but in all the other cases the idea of taking part in a larger project, especially where this was national, enhanced the value of the project in the eyes of the student (Henry, 1978a). The architecture students were delighted that their work was deemed valuable enough to be saved for posterity. The research methods students wanted to know the results for their region and how this compared to national data and those obtained in previous years.

Mauger *et al.* (1990) report on an annual research seminar which gives pharmacy undergraduates from all over the Eastern USA a chance to present the findings from their undergraduate research projects. A survey of the 22 colleges who had taken part suggested a high standard of work: a third of participants went on to publish and a half to pursue graduate study in pharmacy.

Attitude

It seems that while some students welcome project work, others find this approach much less conducive to their natural style. I tried to identify what the key differences were in some of my early research. I presented a series of attitude statements to students which were subsequently subjected to a factor analysis (Henry, 1978b). The first four factors of my 'attitude to projects' scale produced logically reasonable factors relating to the degree of structure, amount of contact, a desire for regularity versus irregularity and concern with the relevance and practical work. The variables which correlate with these factors at .4 or above are shown below (note, however, that the first six factors only accounted for 33 per cent of the variance):

Factor 1. Degree of structure
.8   I find course work more interesting than project work
.7   Course units teach you more than projects

.5   You learn more from a structured than unstructured course
.4   I like to know exactly what I'm supposed to be doing
.4   I am reluctant to do projects because of the risk involved.

Factor 2. Amount of contact
.7   I like to be left on my own to sort things out
-.7 I'd like more face-to-face tuition
.6   Tutorials are a waste of time
-.6 It makes all the difference if you have a good tutor.

Factor 3. Regularity versus irregularity
.8   I always hand in my assignments on time
-.8 I am usually behind with my work
.5   I tend to study at set times.

Factor 4. Concern with relevance and practical work
.7   You cannot understand things properly without first-hand experience
.6   Education should deal with real-life problems.

Those not liking projects appeared to prefer 'highly structured teaching materials and directed tutorials and had regular study patterns whereas the obverse was true for those liking projects' (Henry, 1978a).

There was relatively little variation between courses, suggesting the statements measured general attitudes and were not too conditioned by the students' experience of the project (though there was a difference in the unstructured and structured medians on some statements; for instance, on 'wanting more face-to-face tuition', the unstructured median was about two-thirds and the structured nearer a half). One statement in particular is of interest, in its own right: a median of 54 per cent said they were 'usually behind with their work': (Henry, 1978a)!

Project work may appeal more to certain cognitive styles than others. Project work requires deep-level processing – attending to the big picture or main point, rather than simply a surface-level approach – focusing more on reproducing detail (Marton and Saljo, 1976). One might expect those favouring a surface-level approach to have a less favourable attitude to project work than those favouring a deep-level approach.

Research on the motivation of students who opt to study alone has highlighted the appeal of flexibility as well as subject-area interest. For example, Penland's (1977) American research suggested that the main reasons students opted to study alone were a positive desire to study flexibly at their own pace, in their own style, to put their own structure on the project and wanting to start immediately rather than being unable to pay the cost of a conventional class or having problems getting there. Coopers and Lybrand (1989) also concluded that the main reasons for the appeal of open and distance learning were factors such as flexible study times and the absence of the need to be away from work.

Take-up

The OU study found that well over four-fifths of OU students who had taken a course which included a project said they would do a project course again, so the gross overload had obviously not put off most students. Furthermore, when asked whether they preferred courses with or without project work, on all but three courses the majority stated they preferred courses with project work. On the three largest unstructured projects, over two-thirds preferred courses with a project to those without. Students were also asked whether they would like to see more project work in courses; just over half felt the number should remain the same. Of the remainder, on most courses these were more students who wanted more projects in courses, than there were students who wanted less. However, students concerned about workload are less likely to prefer or favour project work.

Since students derive most benefit from the largest unstructured courses, one might imagine project credits – where the whole course is based round a project – are a valuable addition to the course profile. However, the appeal of courses consisting entirely of projects has been limited at the Open University; while they are popular with students who take them, relatively few are attracted to so doing. A minority jump at the chance and blossom; others stay well clear if given the option. The OU study found the proportion who thought the project credit idea attractive ranged from over two-thirds of students who had experience of a large project to under a fifth of those who were undertaking smaller projects. Anecdotal evidence suggests that one of the inhibiting factors is that students feel they get relatively little for their money with a project credit, since the course fee pays for extra tuition and the students receive much less in the way of course material than they normally would with an open learning course.

However, where students had been asked to pursue a number of different projects within a single course, I found many students wanted to pursue fewer projects in greater depth.

Drop out

There has been some suggestion that the drop out rate of students undertaking project work is slightly higher than normal. The OU study found that, on the contrary, the percentage dropping out of project courses was no worse or better than on other courses, as about half the project courses studied had a lower drop out rate than the average for their faculty and level, and a half had a higher drop out rate. Indeed performance was considerably better than average on some but not all of the courses containing a high proportion of project work (Henry, 1978b, p.132). However, drop out has remained relatively high on projects requiring statistics from non-specialists (eg, educators rather than statistics students).

Once started, the majority of students do go on to complete their projects and of those that fail to, most never seriously begin the work. I found that of the small number of students who begin projects but fail to complete them, field projects had the highest drop out at the data collection stage.

However, if the project is not compulsory a substantial minority may opt to take the easy path and undertake an alternative and easier assignment. Something between a third and a half of students on Open University courses with an optional project have decided against completing it on some courses. Similarly, on some project courses, about a half have not bothered to complete all the project assignments where they are not all necessary for assessment purposes. Needless to say, where these are staged, it is the assignments relating to analysis and the final report that are more likely to be dropped than the project plan.

The most common reasons given for not completing a project include:

- pressure of work
- personal reasons
- shortage of time.
- ceasing to work on the course
- getting behind

Other factors include:

- difficulty in obtaining information
- moving house
- starting too late
- having submitted enough other assignments.

It is interesting to note that of the OU post-experience students who dropped out, a quarter were 'unhappy with their work' and nearly a fifth of students who failed to complete on two other courses pointed out 'other assignments were easier' (Henry, 1978b, pp.172, 174, 266).

For most students it was a combination of one or more factors that led to them failing to finish the project work. Nevertheless, if we can believe them, these responses are encouraging, since the most common factors are unrelated to the project work.

However, the overload problem and importance of starting early are highlighted by those who failed because of the time problems. Unlike most other course material, it is not usually possible to catch up on project work by a period of concentrated study because of the time needed to arrange access, wait for material and organize special trips out of work hours. The tutor must always feel concern for the minority who failed to finish the work because of difficulty in obtaining information; this applied to over a fifth of students on a quarter of the OU project courses. Some projects may need redesigning to make it easier for students to obtain the information or by providing a fall-back project for students who have great difficulty in finding sufficient data.

Certain projects have higher drop out rates. For example, projects involving statistical analysis often have a higher drop out rate than those that do not. Courses with a quantitative, computing and/or statistical component, like research methods and cognitive psychology, often have higher drop out rates than other non-quantitative social science courses. The pressure is sometimes exacerbated in such projects as a student has to be able to understand the material more thoroughly so as to apply it to a project.

Concurrent projects

Staff are sometimes suspicious of students undertaking one or more project courses simultaneously, advancing the hypothesis that the canny student can use the same project for different courses. Students, on the other hand, often find taking two or more projects simultaneously makes their general course load much more difficult. In the OU study this was true of four-fifths of those studying unstructured projects and three-fifths of those taking a structured project (Henry, 1978b, pp.137–8). (In fact over half the students taking two or more courses containing project work failed to sit the exam for one or more of the courses.)

The load is increased where project assignments are due in at similar times. Staff often place project work at the end of a course. Where many students are doing two or more courses with projects concurrently, shifting one of these to a different point in the course and phasing assignment due dates may dramatically improve performance in both.

Review

Despite the difficulties and workload involved in projects, the level of interest generated by project work is phenomenally high. The majority of students find project work very interesting, very worthwhile and a very useful part of the course.

Far from balking at the responsibility involved in conducting a project, students find it is the challenge that accounts for the appeal of projects. Many students welcome the opportunity to use their initiative in tackling a project of their own choosing and most report a sense of achievement at having risen to the task. The largest unstructured projects produce the most enthusiastic students, and students on unstructured projects generally find the work more satisfying than those on structured projects. Students often become more competent and more confident after completing a project.

Reaction to project work is variable. Some students seem to come into their own with this kind of work. Indeed, a higher percentage of those who opt to take project courses prefer courses with projects to those without, and want more, rather than less, project work in their courses, but this is a self-selected sample. While most students are prepared to undertake project work again, it has to be said that some students really do not like the responsibility entailed and prefer a more structured curriculum.

While most people think a project credit is a desirable component in an undergraduate degree and a necessary one in an honours degree, given the freedom to choose whether or not to take that route, often only a minority opt to take the project credit. Those that do often find the experience much more rewarding than their other educational studies.

There is some evidence to suggest that dropout on courses including project work is similar to those without. Most students do finish their project. The most common reasons given for dropping out are personal and unconnected with the project, but getting behind and time problems are also important. Relatively few students cite difficulty in obtaining information as a reason for failing to complete the project. Perhaps teachers could incorporate fall-back options for such students, and check the availability of material or modify projects where a relatively high percentage of students have difficulty locating data.

The vast majority of those taking two or more courses, both or all of which include projects, feel this makes the workload more difficult. This is exacerbated by the fact that projects in different courses are often placed at the same point, ie, at the end of the course.

Points for reflection

Think of a particular project you would like students to do.
What do you expect students to gain from doing this project?
How difficult do you think they will find it?
Given a choice, how many of your students would opt to do this project themselves?
Can you identify some individuals who are likely to find this project less conducive than others? How can you help them?

Appendix: The OU study

The OU project study had two main phases: a qualitative phase involving interviews with 300 students, tutors and academics on ten project courses in three different regions and at residential school; and a quantitative phase comprising a long postal survey sent to a sample of over 4,000 students on 20 project courses. The response rate was 77 per cent. The table below describes some of the features of the projects included in the main study.

	Unstructured projects										
Course:	A305	A401	D301	D331	D332	S323	S333	T262	TAD292	TD342	P853
Assignments	3	2	4	3	2	2	2	2	5	1	2
Time (hrs)	80	160	160	70	36	36	20	50–60	120	30	20
Face-to-face tuition	9	5	15	9	8	0	15	8	25	6	1.5
Residential school	y					y	y		y	y	

	Structured projects								
Course:	D203	D291	D305	E201	E203	E341	PE261	PT272	T351
Assignments	1	5–7	1–3	2	1	1	1	2/3	1
Time (hrs)	24	50–70	10–30	20	10	24–31	21	6	10
Face-to-face tuition	9	0	16	16	16	10	7–9	8.5	19

Where the project was one component in a course, half the courses studied had allocated 50 per cent or more of their course assessments to the project. In 80 per cent of courses studied, the project was compulsory, in the sense that a student failing to submit it received no marks for that assignment.

Acknowledgements

I would like to acknowledge research assistance from Margaret Teft. I would also like to thank the many people who have helped with the various phases of research into the use of project work in open and distance learning, notably project study group members B Crooks, P Davey, P Duchastel, N Farnes, A Morgan and project course team chairs J Bynner, C Crickmay, A Learmonth, J Martin, S Nicolson, R Stevens and M Wilson.

References

Adderley, K *et al.* (1975) *Project Methods in Higher Education*, Guildford: Society for Research in Higher Education Monograph 24.

Allison, J and Benson, FA (1983) 'Undergraduate projects and their assessment', *IEE Proceedings*, **130**, Pt A, 8, November, pp.402–19.

Bates, A (1976) memo quoted in Crooks *et al.* (1977).

Bell, J (1993) *Doing Your Research Project*, Buckingham: Open University Press.

Benson, J and Allinson, FA (1979) 'Undergraduate projects and their assessment', *IEE Proceedings*, **130**, 8, 402–19.

Blacklock, S (1975) *T262 Evaluation*, Survey Research Department IET, Milton Keynes: Open University.

Boud, D (ed.) (1981) *Developing Student Autonomy in Learning*, London: Kogan Page.

Boud, D (1989) 'Some competing traditions in experiential learning' in Warner-Weil and Gibson (1989).

Brennen, JL and Percy, KA (1977) 'What do students want? An analysis of staff and students' perceptions of higher education', in Bonboir A (ed.), *Instructional Design in Higher Education*, European Association for Research and Development in Higher Education Vol 1, pp.125–52.

Bruner, JS (1971) 'The process of education revisited', *Phi Delta Kappa*, September, 18–21, quoted in Morgan, A (1984) 'Project-based learning TCC Report No 8', Milton Keynes: Open University.

Bruner, JS (1977) *The Process of Education*, 2nd edn. Cambridge, Mass: Harvard University Press.

Bynner, J (1975) *E341 Student Survey*, Milton Keynes: School of Education, Open University

Bynner, J and Henry, J (1984) 'Advanced project work in distance teaching' *Higher Education*, **13**, pp.413–21.

Byrne, CJ (1979) 'Tutor marked assignments at the Open University: a question of reliability', *Teaching at a Distance*, **15**, p.34–43.

Carter, G and Lee, LS (1981) 'A sample survey of departments of electrical engineering to ascertain the aims, objectives and methods of assessing first-year undergraduate laboratory work in electronic and electrical engineering', *Journal of Electrical Engineering Education*, **18**, 113–19, quoted in Allison and Benson (1983).

Chambers, R G (1964, 1972) 'A survey of laboratory teaching', *Bulletin of the Institute of Physics and Physics Society*, **15**, 4, 77–84.

Chambers, R G (1972) 'Supplementary notes to "Laboratory Teaching in the United Kingdom" ', in *New Trends in Physics Teaching*, Vol II, UNESCO, Paris, quoted in Asden, P and Eardley, B (1974) *Teaching Practical Physics: The Open University and Other Approaches*, Milton Keynes: Faculty of Science, Open University.

Coopers and Lybrand (1989) *A Report into the Relative Costs of Open Learning*, London: Open University/Dept of Employment.

Cornwall, M (1975) 'Authority versus experience in Higher Education', *Universities Quarterly*, **29**, 3.

Cornwall, M *et al.* (eds) (1977) *Project Orientation in Higher Education*, University of Brighton/University of London Institute of Education.

Crooks, B, Davey, P, Duchastel, P, Henry, J and Morgan, A (1977) *Project Work: Brief case studies*, Project Study Group Memo 2 IET, Milton Keynes: Open University.

Cross, N and Ransome, S (1977) 'Survey of a project-based course', *Teaching at a Distance*, 8, 59–61:

Dewey, J (1916) *Democracy and Education*, New York: Macmillan.

Dirckinck-Holmfeld, L (1991) 'Making project pedagogy function in distance learning through the use of computer conferencing', in Lorensen, A and Komos, A (eds) *Quality by Theory and Practice in Higher Education*, Technology and New Pedagogy No 6, University of Aalborg.

Dressel, P L and Thompson, M M (1973) *Independent Study*, San Francisco, CA: Jossey-Bass.

Duchastel, P (1976) 'TAD292 – Art and environment and its challenge to educational technology', *Programmed Learning and Educational Technology*, **13**, 4, 61–5.

Edwards, D (1979) *Project Marking*, Student Assessment Report Group Research Paper, Milton Keynes: IET, Open University.

Edwards, D (1982) 'Project marking: Some problems and issues', *Teaching at a Distance*, **21**, 28–36.

Even, M J (1982) 'Adapting cognitive style theory in practice', *Lifelong learning: The adult years*, **5**, 5, 14–16, 27, quoted in Brockett, RG and Hiemstra, R 'Bridging the theory – practice gap in self-directed learning', in Brookfield, S (ed.) (1985) *Self-directed Learning: From theory to practice*, New Directions in Continuing Education No 25, San Francisco, CA: Jossey-Bass, p.32

Fail, J L (1991) 'The value of student-originated and student-run ecology projects', *American Biology Teacher*, **53**, 3, 170.

Fruensgaard, NF (1991) 'Project work as a study technique at Aalborg University', in Lorentsen, A and Kolmos, A (eds) *Quality by Theory and Practice of Higher Education*, Technology and New Pedagogy No 6, Aalborg, Denmark: Aalborg University, pp.216–23.

Gains, D (1977) *Libraries for Project Courses – Pilot study*, Yorkshire Region, Open University.

Gallagher, M (1977) *Broadcasting and Open University Students*, Milton Keynes: IET, Open University.

Gault, JW and Synder, WE (1978) 'An undergraduate design project course utilising a microcomputer, *IEEE Transcripts*, **E-22**, 138–42.

Gibbons, M (1984) 'Walkabout ten years later: Searching for a new vision of education', *Phi Delta Kappen*, **65**, 9, 591–600, quoted in Metzger (1988–9).

Gorb, P (1987) 'Projects not cases: teaching design to managers', *Management Education and Development*, **18**, 4, 299–307.

Greene, J and D'Oliveira, M (1982) *Learning to Use Statistical Tests in Psychology: A students guide*, Buckingham: Open University Press.

Gull, H (1993) *Projects in the Education of Young Children*, London: McDougall (quoted in Adderley, 1975).

Hawkins, J (1980) *London Region Library Listing*, London: Open University.

Helms, M and Haynes, P (1990) 'When bad groups are good: an appraisal of learning and group projects', *Journal of Education for Business*, **66**, 1, 5–8.

Henderson, E and Nathenson, M (1984) *Independent Learning in Higher Education*,

Englewood Cliffs, NJ: Educational Technology Publications.

Henry, JA (1977a) 'The course tutor and project work', *Teaching at a Distance*, **9**.

Henry, JA (1977b) 'A study of project work at the Open University', paper presented to the Association of Institutional Researchers Annual Forum, Montreal, Canada.

Henry, JA (1978a) *The Project Report. Volume I: Findings and recommendations*, Project Study Group, Milton Keynes: IET, Open University, p.270.

Henry, JA (1978b) *The Project Report. Volume II: The tables*, Project Study Group, Milton Keynes: IET, Open University, p.350.

Henry, JA (1984) 'Projects components in a research methods course' in Henderson and Nathenson (1984).

Henry, JA (1986) *Evaluation of a Project-based Course*, Project Study Group Report No 18, Milton Keynes: IET, Open University.

Henry, JA (1987) 'Experiential learning at a distance', paper presented to the 1st International Experiential Learning Conference, Regents College, London, Teaching and Consultancy Centre Report No. 58, Milton Keynes: IET, Open University.

Henry, JA (1989a) 'Meaning and practice in experiential learning', in Warner-Weil and Gibson (1989).

Henry, JA (1989b) *Low Cost Courses*, Teaching and Consultancy Centre Report No. 5, Milton Keynes: IET, Open University.

Henry, JA (1990) 'The human side of project work', in Eastcote, D and Farmer, B (eds) *Making Learning Systems Work*, London: Kogan Page.

Henry, JA (1992) *Creative Management Evaluation*, Project Report No 32, Milton Keynes: IET, Open University.

Henry, JA (1993) 'Resources and constraints in open and distance learning', in Lockwood, F (ed.) *Materials Production in Open and Distance Learning*, London: Paul Chapman.

Hilton-Jones, U (1988) 'Project-based learning for foreign students in an English-speaking environment', paper presented to 22nd Annual Meeting of Teachers of English as a Foreign Language, Edinburgh.

Hoare, DE (1980) 'Survey of project work in Chemistry degree courses', appendix in *A report on project work in chemistry degree courses*, Royal Society of Chemistry Assessment Group report presented to the University of Aston October meeting.

Hodgson, BK and Murphy, PJ (1984) 'A CAL-based distance education project in evolution: 2. Evaluation of the CAL-based project in relation to alternative projects', *Journal of Biological Education*, **18**, 141–6.

Hotel and Catering Training Company (1993) *Choosing a Work Based Project*, London: Hotel and Catering Training Company.

Howard, K and Sharpe, JA (1983) *The Management of a Student Research Project*, Aldershot: Gower.

Howson, G et al. (1981) *Curriculum Development in Mathematics*, Cambridge: Cambridge University Press, quoted in Zand, H (1984) *Real Problems in Mathematics*, op.cit..

Hunter-Brown, C and Brown, S (1993) *The Management Project: Information search guide*, Buckingham: Open University Press.

Jackson, EA (1987) 'The importance and assessment of final year projects: case studies from Africa', *Assessment and Evaluation in Higher Education*, **12**, 2, 83–93.

Jankowicz, AD (1991) *Business Research Projects for Students*, London: Chapman and Hall.

Katz, LG and Chard, SD (1992) 'The project approach' in Johnson, JE and Roopnarine, J (eds) *Approaches to Early Childhood Education*, Columbus, OH: Merrill Publishing.

Kauffmann, G (1991) 'Problem solving and creativity', in Henry, J (ed.) *Creative*

Management, London: Sage.

Kennedy, CJ (1982) 'Process and product in higher education: student-directed learning', *Journal of Further and Higher Education*, **6**, 3, 56–68.

Kilpatrick, WH (1918) 'The project method', *Teacher's College Record*, **19**, pp319–35.

Koeller, S (1984) 'Challenging language experiences: The project approach versus "reeling and writhing"', *Childhood Education*, May–June, 331–5.

Kohlberg, L and Mayer, R (1972) 'Development as the aim of education', *Harvard Educational Review*, **42**, 4, 447–96.

Knowles, M (1975) *Self-directed Learning: A guide for learners and teachers*, New York: Cambridge Book.

Kroll, L (1985) 'Teaching the research process via organic chemistry lab projects', *Journal of Chemical Education*, **62**, 5.

Litogoy, S (1991) 'Using higher-order skills in American history', *Social Studies*, Jan/Feb, **82**, 1, 22–5.

Lupton, K (1976) 'The project-syllabus method in experiential education', *Alternative Higher Education: The Journal of Non-Traditional Education*, **1**, 1, 43–50.

Mace, E (1975) *A305 evaluation*, Milton Keynes: IET, Open University.

Mace, E (1984) 'A project component in architectural history', in Henderson and Nathenson (1984).

Mangham, IL (1986) 'In search of competence', *Journal of General Management*, **12**, 2, 5–12.

Marton, F and Saljo, R (1976) 'On qualitative differences in learning: Outcome and process', *British Journal of Educational Technology*, **46**, 4–11.

Mauger, K *et al.* (1990) 'An evaluation of the impact of an undergraduate research seminar', *American Journal of Pharmaceutical Education*, **54**, Spring, 43–5.

Melling, J (1972) *Review of decision-making project*, Milton Keynes: Social Science Faculty, Open University.

Metzger, DJ (1988–9) 'Practicing what we preach: Involving student teachers in their learning', *Action in Teacher Education*, **x**, 4, 15–18.

Morgan, A (1980) *Project Based Learning*, Milton Keynes: IET, Open University, Teaching and Consultancy Centre Monograph No 8.

Murrell, J (1975) 'Making reliability' (personal communication).

Olsen, J and Laursen, E (1991) Personal communication.

Packham, R, Roberts, R and Barden, R (1989) 'Our Faculty goes experiential', in Warner-Weil and Gibson (1989).

Paton, R (1990) 'Tutoring managers: The use of experience-based assignments', *Open Learning*, **5**, 3, 28–34.

Paton, R and Lay, C (1986) 'Learning to manage and managing to learn', *Open Learning*, **1**, 3.

Penland, PR (1977) *Self-planned Learning in America*, Pittsburgh, PA: University of Pittsburgh.

Percy, K and Ramsden, P (1980) *Independent Study: Two examples from English higher education*, Guildford: Society for Research in Higher Education.

Philips, E (1981) 'Learning to do research', paper presented to the Artificial Intelligence and Simulated Behaviour Autumn School.

Ramsden, P (1977) 'The North East London Polytechnic Dip. HE Independent Studies Programme', unpublished Ph.D, Lancaster University.

Riley, MW (1980) 'Phases encountered in a project team', *IEEE Transcript*, **E-23**, 212–3, quoted in Allison and Benson (1983).

Rogers, CR (1969) *Freedom to learn*, Columbus, OH: Merrill.

Samuel, AE (1986) 'Student centered teaching in engineering design', *Instructional Science*, **15**, 213–38.

Schuldt, BA (1991) '"Real-world" versus "simulated" projects in database instruction', *Journal of Education for Business*, Sep/Oct, **67**, 1, 35–9.

Sexton, C (1990) 'A comparative analysis of the project methods and learning project', *International Journal of Lifelong Education*, **9**, 2, 81–98.

Sims, GD (1976) 'Electronic engineers education and the future', *Journal of the Royal Signals Institution*, **12**, 149–72.

Singletary, M and Crook, J (1986) 'Projects replace theses in many master's programs', *Journalism Educator*, winter, **40**, 4, 4–6.

Spear, R (1977) 'A full-credit project in technology', *Teaching at a Distance*, 8, 54–8.

Stephenson, J. (1983) 'Higher education: School for Independent Study', in Tight, M (ed.) *Adult Learning and Education*, Beckenham: Croom Helm, pp.169–86.

Sunderland, J and Toncheva, E (1991) 'The value of project work in INSET', paper presented to the 24th Annual Meeting of the International Association of English as a Foreign Language, Dublin.

Swift, B (1992) *MBA Quality Audit*, Student Research Centre, Bucks: Open University.

Swift, J (1726/1974) *Gulliver's Travels*, Oxford: Oxford University Press.

Thorpe, M (1977) 'Evaluating Tutorial Attendance', *Teaching at a Distance*, 10.

Tough, AM (1967) *Learning Without a Teacher: A study of tasks and assistance during adult self-teaching projects*, Ontario: Ontario Institute for Studies in Education.

Tough, AM (1979) *The Adult's Learning Projects: A fresh approach to theory and practice in adult learning*, 2nd edn., San Diego: University Associates, and Ontario: Ontario Institute for Studies in Education.

Tough, AM (1985) 'Self directed learning: concepts and practice', in *International Encyclopaedia of Education: Research and Studies*, **8**, pp.4511–15.

University of Surrey Course Staff (1984) *Advice Before Starting a Project*, Module P, Diploma in the Practice of Higher Education, Guildford: Institute of Educational Technology, University of Surrey.

Usher, JR, Simmonds, DG and Earl, SE (1991) 'Industrial enhancement through problem based learning', in Boud, D and Feletti, G (eds) *Problem based learning*, London: Kogan Page.

USMES (1976) *The USMES Guide*, Newton, Mass: Education Development Center, 4th edn, quoted in Zand (1984).

Varley, P (1975) 'Ecology projects: An innovation', *Teaching at a Distance*, **1**, 2.

Warner-Weil, S and Gibson, I (eds) (1989) *Making Sense of Experiential Learning: Diversity in theory and practice*, Guildford: SHRE/OU Press.

Whitehead, JS (1981) 'Denmark's two university centres: The quest for stability, autonomy and distinctiveness', *Higher Education*, **10**, 89–101.

Zand, H (1984) '"Real Problem" projects in mathematics', in Henderson and Nathenson (1984).

Index